BROKENNESS
and the
STRONG MAN'S GOSPEL

Parallel Tracks to Access God's Power

JERRY GRIESER

Copyright © 2015 by Jerry Grieser

Brokenness and the Strong Man's Gospel
Parallel Tracks to Access God's Power
by Jerry Grieser

Printed in the United States of America.

ISBN 9781498437042

All rights reserved solely by the author. The author guarantees all contents are original and do not infringe upon the legal rights of any other person or work. No part of this book may be reproduced in any form without the permission of the author. The views expressed in this book are not necessarily those of the publisher.

Unless otherwise indicated, Scripture quotations taken from the New American Standard Bible (NASB). Copyright © 1960, 1962, 1963, 1968, 1971, 1972, 1973, 1975, 1977, 1995 by The Lockman Foundation. Used by permission. All rights reserved.

www.xulonpress.com

Contents

Introduction vii

1. The Paradox 9
2. To Tie Up a Strong Man 15
3. Is There Victory in God? 21
4. Should God's Victory Characterize the Believer's Walk? 27
5. To What Lineage Do We Belong? 31
6. What Kind of People does the Gospel Turn Men and Women Into? 35
7. What Does God Expect the Strong Man's Gospel to Do? 39
8. How Do We Demonstrate the Strong Man's Gospel in our Life? 45
9. What is God Waiting For? 57
10. How Do We Take Possession of the Power of God? . . 65
11. How Do We Prevent the Marking Off of Boundaries? . 75
12. What's in a Name, Anyway? 81
13. Excuse Me? 87

Introduction

God's Word tells us that as New Creation men and women we have been birthed by God. Many verses speak of our new-found nobility and of God's Spirit touching our spirit. Others describe His energy, even His very nature flowing through us. Still others paint a picture of victory, even extreme victory, characterizing our lives. This information should make us strong in faith, causing us to step out and act courageously. But most believers' lives don't appear empowered. I believe there are two reasons we fail to experience this kind of life. The first is lack of revelation. As we develop in our revelation of Who dwells in us, and understand our true nobility, we will begin to radiate the victory just described. When this happens, people will be able to see God's glory and His presence in us. We will have embraced the strong man's gospel and employed its benefits in our life.

A lack of brokenness, a lack of total dependency on God and His strength, is the second reason we fail to see this victory. We attempt to "do things for God" in our own strength and with our own talents and thus end up far short of the picture painted in God's Word. This attempt at demonstrating the strong man's gospel produces a counterfeit form of the gospel

Jesus came to bring and its pretension is clearly seen by the world. Brokenness is an integral part of authentically operating in the strong man's gospel.

Similar to the rails on which a train rides, brokenness and the strong man's gospel are parallel tracks we must journey together for the effectiveness of either to be fully realized. The premise of the strong man's gospel is to use God's finger to beat Satan at his own game, to destroy his arsenal of weapons. This can only happen through brokenness. Our own abilities, strengths, and talents must be "set aside" in order for the picture of the strong man's gospel to impact us. This gospel is *in us,* but as long as we hold onto what *we* can do, we will not allow God to paint for us a picture of *His power* flowing through us.

Brokenness and the Strong Man's Gospel will help you begin to understand your union with your Creator. It will show you what you can do to begin demonstrating the strong man's gospel in your life. It will help you understand what it is that gives evidence or proof of the Living One who was dead but is now alive forevermore. In it you will find where your responsibility lies in operating in the strong man's gospel. And the excuses we use for not embracing either brokenness or the strong man's gospel will be exposed for what they are, mere excuses. *Brokenness and the Strong Man's Gospel* will encourage you to drop them and move forward.

My prayer for you is that *Brokenness and the Strong Man's Gospel* might inspire you to take possession of the power of God and tie up the enemy using God's finger to beat Satan at his own game. I pray that the picture of victory painted in God's Word may characterize your life.

Jerry

1.

The Paradox

Brokenness and the Strong Man's Gospel is the result of a conversation I had with God while I was on the road to brokenness and ministering on that subject. What I mean by "conversation" is simply a heart to heart discussion, God speaking to my heart and mine answering to His. That conversation went like this;

"God, what is it that you want me to teach?"

"The Strong Man's Gospel!" He said.

"Excuse me? I'm on the road to brokenness right now, God," I answered.

"Exactly!" He said.

"Lord, the message I've been getting from you is one of repentance, of getting down, dipping like Namman in the dirty Jordan River," I answered questioningly.

"Exactly!" is all I heard.

"Lord, I feel that you have been taking me out into the wilderness, stripping me of my dependence on self, friends, abilities, talents, desires, egos, and agendas. I feel that at this time I'm experiencing a spiritual wilderness, a time of developing total dependency on you," I responded.

Once again the Lord said, "Exactly!"

"Lord, it seems a **paradox** to me, to minister brokenness, giving it up, breaking the vial and waiting upon you, and then speak on stepping out, rising up, pressing in, expecting, and taking hold," I challenged.

"It is not," He stated.

"Lord, it is not a paradox?" I asked.

"No!" He answered.

And then I heard His heart in the matter. He said, "I don't want my children to mistake brokenness for weakness. I don't want them to mistake waiting for passivity. I don't want them to mistake meekness for paralysis. And I don't want them to mistake dependence for laziness."

"So, You want us to simultaneously learn from our wilderness experiences, our brokenness and our vulnerability, while at the same time learning how to embark on the journey of the "The Strong Man's Gospel?" I asked.

"Yes!" He answered.

**Don't Mistake Brokenness for weakness,
Waiting for passivity, Meekness for paralysis,
Dependence for laziness.**

It definitely isn't the way I would have done it, but most of the time I'm pretty sure God knows better than me. So, I made a choice to do it His way regardless of the outcome. It doesn't matter if it seems a paradox to me. For the Guy who told me to go down this seemingly paradoxical road of brokenness and the strong man's gospel is the same Guy who said, "Be firm, yet flexible." He is the One Who said, "Take no thought what you will eat or drink or wear," and then said, "He who does not work does not eat."

He says, "Walk by faith, not by sight," and then tells us He is our high priest who is able to understand, sympathize, and have a shared **feeling** with our weaknesses. He exhorts us, "Judge not, lest you be judged," then tells us to "judge all things." He asks us to "bear one another's burdens," then tells us that "each man should bear his own load." He declares, "I am the prince of peace who gives you peace," then says, "I did not come to bring peace but a sword, to turn a mother against her daughter, a father against his son, a son against his father."

"Faith alone will save you," He says, then tells us that saving faith is never alone. This is the same God who revealed to us the law and then gave us grace, telling us grace is what we are to live in. He is the One Who elected us and yet gave us each a free will! This is the God who says He is One, and Three, and Seven, and yes, even male and female!

<u>We serve a God of seeming paradoxes, but we have a Spirit who harmonizes all these seeming contradictions!</u>

He is the one who said in Matthew 13:52 that the new is in the old contained, but that the old is in the new explained! He is the one who tells me that I am saved, am being saved, and will be saved, a great paradox of its own! He is the Second Man, Adam, from Whom was extracted His bride, poured out in the blood and the water from His sword pierced side, a human sword, itself a paradox to the living sword which extracted Eve!

This is why I choose to do it His way. I am in awe of the seeming paradox of my God and me, the Creator and the created, yet we are one! The paradox of paradoxes! He is compassionate, yet tough. He is trusting. He trusts me with His name, with His Spirit, and yet He is demanding. He is consistent, yet flexible. He caters to the curiosity of Thomas, letting him touch and see, while commending a gentile centurion for believing blindly.

This is why I desire to teach as He instructs! I will do it in the face of my own fears that I will be confronted with the seeming contradictions of waiting and moving, of crying and shouting, of gentleness and firmness, of humility and victory, of sorrow and joy, of human loneliness and godly unity.

There is some mystery in all of this, and while we do well to pursue an understanding of God, it behooves us not to attempt to erase the mystery of God. If we could erase the mystery of God, if we could explain Him, then we would be God's god! He cannot be explained. He can only be revealed. David didn't try to explain Him. He simply revealed Him in Psalm 24:8-10, *"Who is the King of Glory? The Lord strong and mighty, the Lord mighty in battle. Lift up your heads, O gates, and lift them up, O ancient doors, that the King of glory may come in! Who is this king of glory? The Lord of hosts, He is the King of glory."*

I lift up my head and say, "Come in, Lord of glory. I'll do it Your way." I would have waited until I was out of the wilderness before taking hold of the strong man's gospel, for in my mind we are unprepared for it until we have experienced the total stripping away of self in the wilderness. But God says we need it **in** the wilderness. God says we can operate in the "strong man's gospel" in the midst of brokenness, in the sorrow of repentance, and in the barrenness of the desert! He says we need it! He says the Israelites had it, didn't always use it, but it was what brought them through!! Moses and Joshua presented the "strong man's gospel" to them and led them to victory in the midst of a very negative situation, their wilderness.

Apparently the "strong man's gospel" is not a paradox of brokenness, but actually a parallel to it. I believe God wants us to parallel the strong man's gospel alongside our trek through the wilderness as we experience the brokenness and repentance that God has designed to show forth His glory, glory He has poured into us. With God having articulated it to me in this manner, I combined the messages of *Brokenness and the Strong Man's Gospel*. This book is not about brokenness, nor is it about the strong man's gospel. This book is about brokenness *and* the strong man's gospel.

2.

To Tie Up a Strong Man

By this time you may be asking, "What exactly is this strong man's gospel?" The strong man's gospel is living in God's power and victory, living free from Satan's influence, and employing all the benefits of God's power. Jesus spoke of the strong man's gospel when he responded to the Pharisees accusation that He cast out demons by Beelzebul, the ruler of demons, in Matthew 12:28-29 (The Message); *"But if it's by God's power that I am sending the evil spirits packing, then God's kingdom is here for sure. How in the world do you think it's possible in broad daylight to enter the house of an <u>awake, able-bodied man and walk off with his possessions unless you tie him up first</u>? Tie him up, though, and you can clean him out."*

What does it take to tie up a strong man? A stronger man! It takes a **stronger** man to tie up a strong man in broad daylight when he can see you coming! Luke's rendition of Jesus' response paints a picture of how brokenness **does** parallel this strong man's gospel. **Luke 11:17-23** (The Message); *"Jesus knew what they were thinking and said, 'Any country in civil* *war for very long is wasted. **A constantly squabbling family falls to pieces**. If Satan cancels Satan, is there any Satan left? You accuse me of ganging up with the Devil, the prince of demons, to cast out demons, but if you're slinging devil mud at me, calling me a devil who kicks out devils, doesn't the same mud stick to your own exorcists? **<u>But if it's God's finger I'm pointing that sends the demons on their way</u>**, then God's kingdom is here for sure. When a **<u>strong man</u>**, armed to the teeth, stands guard in his front yard, his property is safe and sound. **<u>But what if a stronger man comes along with superior weapons?</u>** Then he's beaten at his own game, the arsenal that gave him such confidence hauled off, and his precious possessions plundered. This is war, and there is no neutral ground. If you're not on my side, you're the enemy; if you're not helping, you're making things worse.'"*

This tells us we are not going to move forward using Satan's tactics, for Satan's tactics do not produce brokenness. If in our marriage, ministry, or relationships we use Satan's tactics of manipulation, the silence game, passivity, signals, or body language to send a message, we will not progress. There will be no progress, for Satan does not cancel Satan. If we attempt to employ Satan's tactics to achieve our goals, to set the record straight, or to press forward our agenda, we will fall to pieces! Matthew, in The Message, said, "A constantly squabbling family **disintegrates**."

Jesus is teaching us how to beat the enemy at his own game. We will not realize the benefits of "strong man warfare with superior weapons" if we are employing the arsenal of Satan's finger, his tactics! Instead of employing Satan's arsenal, we are to use God's finger to beat Satan at his own game, destroy the arsenal that gives him confidence in our lives, and retrieve the precious possessions that he has taken so deceptively from us. Satan has stolen from us the precious possessions of oneness, unity, joy, passion, love, peace, victory, and expectancy. God placed within us a spirit of expectancy and Satan does everything he can to suck it out of us. Satan steals oneness and unity from our marriages with deception. He gets us to focus on the physical dimension, look around at others' mates, and conclude that our own just does not measure up. "Your spouse doesn't have what you need," he says, deceptively destroying our precious possessions. God's finger would take them all back! But what do we usually do? We use Satan's arsenal to try to retrieve them! But Satan's arsenal does not cancel Satan! Manipulation will not work. Coercion is ineffective. And neither anger nor passivity will be able retrieve the precious possessions of oneness, unity, and passion.

> **We will not realize the benefits of "strong man warfare with superior weapons" if we are employing the arsenal of Satan's tactics!**

Jesus makes it clear that this is war and there is no neutral ground. We cannot be playing around with the enemy's arsenal, using his weapons or methods of attack, and still promote the Kingdom of God! It cannot happen! *"Any country in civil war for very long is wasted!"* Jesus is saying to us, "If you're not on my side, using my weapons, my methods of warfare, then you are the enemy! There is no neutral ground! If you're not helping by using God's finger, His power, then you're making things worse by employing the tactics of my enemy!"

I am convinced that we will not employ God's power to send demons on their way until we are broken of the self-centered desire to elevate ourselves by using the tactics of those very demons. Therefore it may well be that we need to find someone who is already broken to employ the finger of God and drive out that demonic desire! How is that for humbling one's self? But indeed, the first step toward brokenness is admitting the need for help! In my own journey toward brokenness, I found I could do *this*. I could admit my need for help! I could admit to demonic influence and control! This first step, though difficult, was not impossible when I found myself drowning! But the second step is what I found most difficult! Asking for help!!

It is one thing to say, "Yes, I have a problem. Yes, I know I need help." It is yet another thing to say, "Would you help me? Would you point God's finger at me and tie up the strong man in my life? I am tired of him controlling me and I find myself unable to break his desire in me. He has planted in me the desire to use his weapons and I find myself not wanting to let go of them. The weapons have become so familiar to me. They feel so comfortable in my hands. I'm afraid to let them go, and yet I want to! Please help me." The latter is an expression of brokenness! Toward brokenness is the direction we should be heading. Is it a pleasant journey? Not unless we take the attitude of the Psalmist who in Psalm 141:5 said, *"Let the righteous smite me in kindness and reprove me; It is oil upon the head; Do not let my head refuse it...,"* and the poet who in Proverbs 13:18 said; *"Poverty and shame will come to him who neglects discipline, But he who regards reproof will be honored."* This is what is required to authentically operate in the strong man's gospel.

3.

Is There Victory in God?

We have established that brokenness and a regard for discipline and reproof is required to *authentically* operate in the strong man's gospel. It is with this attitude that we must approach the first logical question arising from combining brokenness and the strong man's gospel, "Is there victory in God?" At first, victory and brokenness seem to be antithetical, rather than complimentary. As noted at the beginning, this is a study of how brokenness influences the strong man's gospel and the excuses we use for not operating in it. Ironically, the brokenness that is required for operating authentically in the strong man's gospel is often the number one excuse that is used for not operating in it at all.

On our journey toward brokenness we feel that we have no business or even ability to operate in the strong man's gospel. When we are at the heights of experiencing brokenness, we seldom view victory as an objective to pursue. It seems incongruous. But God wants to shatter that myth by showing us the progressive nature of brokenness. Brokenness never comes overnight. You think you are there, empty, nothing else left of self, and *surprise*, there it is, self, still very much intact! You realize that *self* is extremely thickheaded and rebellious. You realize that *self* will not give up quite so easily.

Gene Edwards in *A Tale of Three Kings* (1980) likens the journey toward brokenness to going to school. In chapter 5 he writes;

> "God has a university. It's a small school. Few enroll, even fewer graduate. Very, very few indeed.
>
> God has this school because He does not have broken men. Instead He has several other types of men. He has men who claim to be God's authority… and aren't; men who claim to be broken… and aren't. And men who *are* God's authority, but who are mad *and* unbroken. And He has, regretfully, a spectroscopic mixture of everything in between. All of these He has in abundance; but broken men, hardly at all.
>
> In God's sacred school of submission and brokenness, why are there so few students? Because all who are in this school must suffer much pain. And as you might guess, it is often the unbroken ruler (whom God sovereignly picks) who metes out the pain. David was once a student in this school, and Saul was God's chosen way to crush David.

3.

Is There Victory in God?

We have established that brokenness and a regard for discipline and reproof is required to *authentically* operate in the strong man's gospel. It is with this attitude that we must approach the first logical question arising from combining brokenness and the strong man's gospel, "Is there victory in God?" At first, victory and brokenness seem to be antithetical, rather than complimentary. As noted at the beginning, this is a study of how brokenness influences the strong man's gospel and the excuses we use for not operating in it. Ironically, the brokenness that is required for operating authentically in the strong man's gospel is often the number one excuse that is used for not operating in it at all.

On our journey toward brokenness we feel that we have no business or even ability to operate in the strong man's gospel. When we are at the heights of experiencing brokenness, we seldom view victory as an objective to pursue. It seems incongruous. But God wants to shatter that myth by showing us the progressive nature of brokenness. Brokenness never comes overnight. You think you are there, empty, nothing else left of self, and *surprise*, there it is, self, still very much intact! You realize that *self* is extremely thickheaded and rebellious. You realize that *self* will not give up quite so easily.

Gene Edwards in *A Tale of Three Kings* (1980) likens the journey toward brokenness to going to school. In chapter 5 he writes;

> "God has a university. It's a small school. Few enroll, even fewer graduate. Very, very few indeed.
>
> God has this school because He does not have broken men. Instead He has several other types of men. He has men who claim to be God's authority... and aren't; men who claim to be broken... and aren't. And men who *are* God's authority, but who are mad *and* unbroken. And He has, regretfully, a spectroscopic mixture of everything in between. All of these He has in abundance; but broken men, hardly at all.
>
> In God's sacred school of submission and brokenness, why are there so few students? Because all who are in this school must suffer much pain. And as you might guess, it is often the unbroken ruler (whom God sovereignly picks) who metes out the pain. David was once a student in this school, and Saul was God's chosen way to crush David.

As the king grew in madness, David grew in understanding. He knew that God had placed him in the king's palace, under true authority.

The authority of King Saul, *true*? Yes, God's chosen authority. *Chosen for David.* Unbroken authority, yes. But divine in ordination, nonetheless.

Yes, *that* is possible.

David drew in his breath, placed himself under his mad king, and moved farther down the path of his earthly hell." (p. 13-14)

Brokenness is developed in God's university. In His school He will show us the *line upon line, precept upon precept* nature of operating in brokenness and the strong man's gospel. I am definitely not through this school; don't know when I will be, if ever. But still, I will write about this school. Some preachers refuse to preach anything they have not lived. If I were to follow that model, I'm afraid I'd have little to teach. So, in the brokenness I *have* experienced, I choose to write what the Word has to speak, whether I've lived up to its challenges or not, for there may be those reading who are more predisposed to rising to the challenges than I. Thus, to refuse to share what I am unable to live, would be to withhold food from someone who is hungry, only because I myself am unable to digest it!

What would we think of such a man? We would call a man like that selfish and proud! We would call him *unbroken*.

God considers the *willingness* over the *performance* and only asks me to share what He has shown me. He told us this in 2 Corinthians 8:10-15 (The Message): *"So here's what I think: The best thing you can do right now is to finish what you started last year and not let those good intentions grow stale. Your heart's been in the right place all along.* **You've got what it takes to finish it up, so go to it**. *Once the commitment is clear, you do what you can, not what you can't.* **The heart regulates the hands.** *This isn't so others can take it easy while you sweat it out.* <u>No, you're shoulder to shoulder with them all the way,</u> **your surplus matching their deficit, their surplus matching your deficit. In the end you come out even**. *As it is written, 'Nothing left over to the one with the most, Nothing lacking to the one with the least.'"*

God tells me to do what I can, not what I can't. He considers my willingness over my performance. So I humble myself and declare that by no means do I imply that I have mastered living *Brokenness and the Strong Man's Gospel*. The truth is I have only just begun to dance around its edges a little here and there, but I eagerly share this food with you in hope that you may digest it more effectively than I and take me with you as you embark on the journey of brokenness and the strong man's gospel!

Since we've *got what it takes to finish it up*, let's *go to it* and answer our first question, "Is there Victory in God?" Most people with an ounce of Word in them would answer with a resounding "Yes!" From Genesis to Revelation God showed Himself strong and victorious in and through the lives of those He found to have faith. Those who understood that they had a covenant with their Creator called on His power over and over again as they faced either giants or giant obstacles in their lives. They understood and took hold of *the strong man's gospel*, the *good news* that God was for them and wanted them to be "strong and courageous" as they took the land He had delivered into their hands.

We are going to look at some of those characters to see what it was that moved them to employ the benefits of *the strong man's gospel,* and how *brokenness* played a relevant role in that move. Many of these men and women, just like us, at first balked at the idea that they were competent or able to operate in this *gospel*. We will examine their excuses, see how they correlate to ours, and discover how God responded to those excuses. We will find out how our excuses impact God's plan for our life, hopefully causing us to *think* the next time we offer Him an excuse.

We will consider Esther (if anyone had an excuse she did), David (even his own dad said, "Who?"), Gideon (head of the Wimps Anonymous Chapter in Canaan who used the *social position excuse* flawlessly), Moses (champion of the *self-doubt excuse*), Joshua (the "We shouldn't have crossed the Jordon River" leader), Elijah (the "I'm the only one bustin' my butt" prophet), Peter (who experienced the "big visions, shattered dreams" excuse), Paul (the "my way or the highway" driver who finally got run over on the Damascus road), and of course, Jesus, the One who trashed every excuse we could ever dream up!!

4.

Should God's Victory Characterize the Believer's Walk?

If you are one who answered, "Is there victory in God?" with a resounding "yes," the next question to be asked is, "Then should not this victory characterize the believer's walk?" Even those with only the slightest interest in *the strong man's gospel* would agree this victory *should* characterize the believer's walk. In our examination of brokenness and the strong man's gospel we are going to find out why it oftentimes does not. We will analyze the *excuses* of the bible characters, as well as our own, to see if these excuses hinder the victory that the Bible shows us we should be experiencing. We will look at **attitude and vision** to see how these hinder victory.

Attitude and vision are often the biggest factors in determining whether victory characterizes our lives. These factors influence us in the following ways;

1. **Attitude**: How we see ourselves, or the *attitude* we have regarding our 'limitations'.

2. **Vision**: The *vision* we have of what we can accomplish.

Vision is the ability to *see* something that is yet unseen.

Attitude and vision are interrelated and interdependent. If our attitude sees insurmountable limitations, it does not matter how large or small our vision is, it will lie dormant. Yet, if we see ourselves as having no limitations, but have no vision, attitude can take us nowhere.

> **Attitude and vision are often the biggest factors in whether victory characterizes our lives**

If attitude and vision are the greatest factors in whether God's victory characterizes our lives, what must we do to adjust our attitude and create a vision conducive to this victory? If we were to look at history and examine the leaders of great conquering nations and kings of vast empires, we would find they had a great sense of who they were, of what they were born into. They believed they were born into greatness, even adding titles to their names depicting as much; Alexander the Great, Herod the Great, Caesar the Great. We could watch any movie in this genre and find that many of these historical leaders and warriors believed they were born for victory, destined to conquer. They knew who they were! Their name was their heritage. The movies often depict a father telling them *who* they are, encouraging and even pushing them to become all that their name was meant to be. The essence of nobility shaped their attitude and built into their psyche a vision of domination and rule.

So if we are to ever adjust our attitude and create a vision conducive to God's victory we must first begin to find out *who* we are, *what* we were born into, and *how* we were destined to live.

5.

To What Lineage Do We Belong?

In 1 Peter 2:9 we find a Father telling us *who* we are, encouraging us to become all that our name and nobility was meant to be; *"But you are A **CHOSEN RACE**, A **royal PRIESTHOOD**, A **HOLY NATION**, A **PEOPLE FOR GOD'S OWN POSSESSION**, so that you may proclaim the excellencies of Him who has called you out of darkness into His marvelous light."*

In Romans 5:17 we hear our Father telling us *what* we were born into, *how* we were destined to live, and over *what* we are to rule; *"For if by the transgression of the one, death reigned through the one, **much more** those who receive the abundance of grace and of the gift of righteousness **will reign in life** through the One, Jesus Christ."*

In this same passage Eugene Peterson in *The Message* implies that our Father pushes us to *grasp with both hands* the destiny to which we were born; *"If death got the upper hand through one man's wrongdoing, can you imagine the breathtaking recovery life makes, **sovereign life**, **in those who grasp with both hands this wildly extravagant life-gift**,* *this grand setting-everything-right, that the one man Jesus Christ provides?"*

Our Father attempts to shape our attitude and build into our psyche, our mind, a vision of domination and rule; *"For if, through the transgression of the one individual, Death made use of the one individual to seize the sovereignty,* **all the more** *shall those who receive God's overflowing grace and gift of righteousness* **reign as kings in Life** *through the one individual, Jesus Christ."* (Weymouth)

Our Father is describing the noble lineage to which we belong! He says to us, "Look at this, you are of noble birth! You have been birthed by Me. You are My own possession! My Spirit has touched your spirit! My energy, My very nature, flows through you. My royal, holy blood flows through your veins! You are destined to reign as kings in Life!"

This alone should make us strong! We need to develop a consciousness, even a vision, of our union with the Almighty, and *grasp with both hands this wildly extravagant life-gift*. Then as we develop in our revelation of Who it is that dwells in us, of our true nobility, we will begin to radiate the victory described in Romans 5:17. Princes and princesses carry themselves with an air of nobility. Our Father desires us to grasp a sense of who we are and carry ourselves in a manner that reflects and radiates our nobility. This is the *sweet aroma* of *triumph in Christ* that Paul spoke of in 2 Corinthians 2:14-16. When we radiate the sweet aroma of Christ's triumph people will be able to see God's glory and His presence in us.

The disciples experienced this aroma of victory after Peter and John were threatened by the religious hierarchy in Acts 4.

Upon release from jail they gathered with the other disciples and began to pray in Acts 4:29-31; *"'And now, Lord, take note of their threats, and grant that Your bond-servants may **speak Your word with all confidence, while You extend Your hand to heal, and signs and wonders take place through the name of Your holy servant Jesus**.' And when they had prayed, **the place where they had gathered together was shaken, and they were all filled with the Holy Spirit and began to speak the word of God with boldness**."*

The disciples were beginning to adjust their attitude and develop a vision for the destiny to which they were born. They were coming to know who they were, or rather *Whose* they were, and saw their nobility as a means to dominate the physical world. Who they were (their nobility) began to radiate from within, the place began to shake, and they were filled with the Holy Spirit, the essence of their Father. In Acts 5:12 and 15-16 we see the results of this adjustment in attitude and expansion of vision; *"And **at the hands of the apostles** many signs and wonders were taking place among the people......to such an extent that they even carried the sick out into the streets, and laid them on cots and pallets, so that when Peter came by, at least his shadow might fall on any of them. And also the people from the cities in the vicinity of Jerusalem were coming together, bringing people who were sick or afflicted with unclean spirits; **and they were all being healed**."*

The disciples altered the physical dimension taking dominion over territory Satan had claimed as his. Their attitude of who they were and the vision of their destiny would not allow them to sit back and watch people suffer, enslaved to tyranny. As princes and princesses of a conquering kingdom they carried themselves with an air of nobility and took possession of territory belonging to their kingdom and set the oppressed free. I believe this is what Paul was talking about in Romans 1:16 when he said *"For I am not ashamed of the gospel, for it* (this almost "too good to be true" gospel) *is **the power of God for salvation to everyone who believes**, to the Jew first and also to the Greek.*

Paul declares that the gospel is the **power** of God! The gospel is more than just information containing good news. It is power, affecting and altering the physical dimension. Revelation of this power influences the attitudes and visions of the people in the Kingdom of God. Using Paul and the New Testament disciples of Christ as examples we discover what kind of people the gospel turns men and women into. The power of God turns men and women into people with attitude! It turns them into people of vision!

> **The gospel is the power of God affecting and altering the physical dimension.**

6.

What Kind of People does the Gospel Turn Men and Women Into?

P aul declared that the gospel is the POWER of God!! It is the power of God creating a New Birth in men and women. This New Birth was not designed by God to make weaklings or pushovers. Remember what God spoke to me concerning the parallel road of brokenness and the strong man's gospel. He said, "Don't mistake brokenness for weakness, waiting for passivity, meekness for paralysis, or dependence for laziness." The New Birth was designed to produce **authentic victory**, not a facade. It was designed to produce a Christian who affects his world, not hide in seclusion behind the walls of a monastery.

David understood *authentic* victory. His attitude of authentic victory is expressed in 2 Samuel 7:18; *"Then David the king went in and sat before the LORD, and he said,* <u>*"Who am I, O Lord GOD, and what is my house, that You have brought me this far*</u>*?"* This is the prayer of a broken man who experienced authentic victory! This is the kind of man the New Birth was designed to produce. The New Birth was designed to produce a race, a *royal race*, of men and women who are strong, bold, and courageous! It was designed to produce heroes. The New Birth was designed to perpetuate the names being added to "Faith's Hall of Fame" in Hebrews 11. It was designed to perpetuate the names of **BROKEN HEROES, BROKEN VICTORS, BROKEN CHAMPIONS, and BROKEN OVERWHELMING CONQUERORS!** The power of God in this New Birth produces broken but authentic warriors for His Kingdom!

Not in the natural, though! Brokenness is not a natural realm phenomenon. Brokenness is only produced through the spiritual dimension. You cannot look at someone's experience and assume they have experienced brokenness. The same events that produce broken victors in some reduce others to broken victims! The difference is the connecting point, not the event! If someone is connected only to the natural realm, regardless of what they experience, it will not produce brokenness. On the other hand, if one is connected to the supernatural realm, he may experience brokenness with or without his experiences. One can experience brokenness responding to God's word without going through a negative circumstance. The connecting point is the issue. The New Birth actually makes a distinction between the natural and the supernatural. In the New Birth, for the first time, one is able to lay aside the natural and draw on the strength and power of the Son of God. This is what is often defined as "the exchanged life." Those who choose to live this exchanged life, laying aside the natural and drawing on the supernatural, are manifesting what God has intended His gospel to be, a "strong man's gospel"! This is what makes a strong man!

A strong man is not someone who simply develops his natural talents and strengths, but one who develops his talents and strengths *for* God's talent and strength to flow through. There is nothing wrong with a pianist developing his or her talent, but it is only when the pianist's talent is developed *for* God's ability to have an avenue to flow through that the pianist becomes a strong man or woman. A weightlifter may develop his muscles for strength, but unless those muscles are developed *for* God's ability to have an avenue to flow through, the weightlifter remains a weak man regardless of how much he can lift.

A strong or talented man, in reference to this strong man's gospel, is not one who simply develops those strengths or talents, but one who develops them *from* the source of God's strength and God's ability. A truly strong or talented man is one who has made the supernatural his connecting point. We must develop our talents *for* <u>HIS</u> ability to have an avenue to <u>FLOW</u> through. The end result of our efforts, whether we are truly strong or weak, will be determined by the *source* of our development. If the source is in the natural, we will remain weak no matter how strong we appear. If the source is in the supernatural, we will become truly strong no matter how weak we appear. This is the essence of *Brokenness and the Strong Man's Gospel*.

A strong man is not someone who works up his courage in the natural, but someone who has laid aside all natural talents and strengths, has plugged totally into God's strength, and is relying solely on His ability. This is what brokenness is. It is quite the opposite of being strong in self-strength. The *strong man's gospel* is only for the one who is able to lay self aside and place a total command on the power of God. This kind of man knows what he can expect from the strong man's gospel! He knows what God designed His gospel to be!

> **The *strong man's gospel* is only for the one who is able to lay self aside and place a total command on the power of God.**

7.

What Does God Expect the Strong Man's Gospel to Do?

The very design of the strong man's gospel is to take what is weak, what is fallen, what is dying (we're talking broken here), and infuse it with supernatural power through the supernatural **connecting point** of the spirit of man. The New Creation Illustration depicts this connection point. The New Birth produces a New Creation being. This is accomplished through the supernatural connecting of man's spirit to the power of God. When the grace of God that has appeared to all men (Titus 2:11) is accepted and received, the power of God (Romans 1:16) flows from the spiritual dimension through the lifeline of faith (Ephesians 2:8) into that man or woman's spirit, infusing it with the very life of God. Everything pertaining to life and godliness (2 Peter 1:3-4), all the resources of heaven, are poured into the spirit of this New Man or Woman. This is where the strong man's gospel resides and this gospel is designed to infuse that which is fallen and weak (the soul), and that which is dying (the body) with supernatural power. As the illustration

Brokenness and the Strong Man's Gospel

reveals, this infusion takes place through the valve on man's spirit called "the will." Yet this valve will never be opened to release the supernatural resources until this New Creation man or woman understands what resides within.

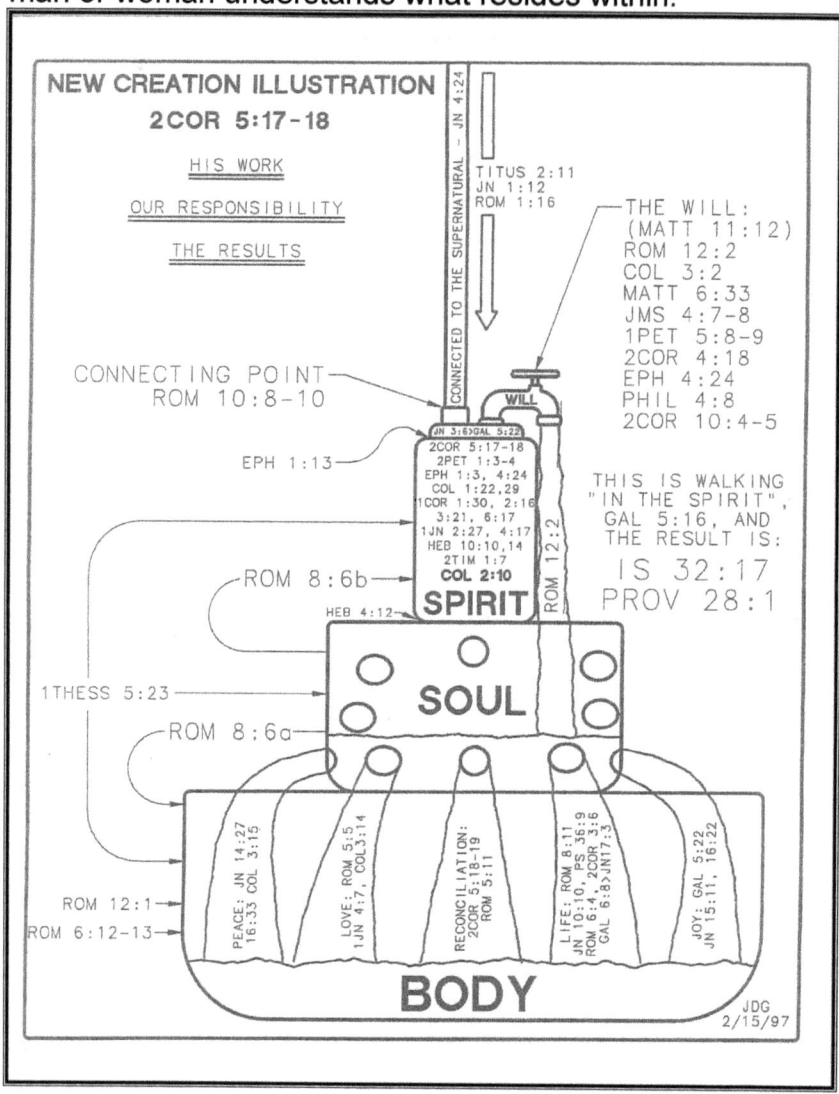

In order for the strong man's gospel to do what God expects it to do, we must get a *picture* of this strong man's gospel, this

power, residing on the inside of us. It is simply a matter of *awareness*! As New Creation men and women we must ask ourselves two questions:
1. Am I aware of the presence of Christ in me?
2. Am I aware of the presence of Christ in me all the time?

Brokenness can produce this awareness. David experienced brokenness and developed a dependency on God as a younVg boy watching his father's sheep alone in the wilderness. His connection to the supernatural and His awareness of God is seen in the many songs he wrote during that time. Years later while being chased around in another wilderness by King Saul, he tapped into this supernatural connection and drew on the power of the strong man's gospel to keep his faith alive and stand on the promise that he would one day be king of Israel. His songs during this time reflect both brokenness and the strong man's gospel. Because of David's connecting point, his wilderness experiences produced brokenness and true strength in his life. It would have destroyed others.

Years later David's brokenness is revealed when Nathan the prophet comes to confront him concerning the cover-up of David's adultery with Bathsheba and the murder of her husband. David's response to Nathan's striking reproof and discipline in the words, "You are that man," displays a heart still connected to God. David lived his life aware that God was with him, and that God was with him all the time. This awareness is what made David a broken victor, a broken champion!

Paul, another broken hero, became keenly aware of Christ residing in him. His blinding experience with Christ on the

Damascus road broke the delusion of self-performance and pride, and connected him to the supernatural realm. When, at the hands of Ananias, the

power of the strong man's gospel hit him, scales fell from his eyes, a revelation of Who Christ was on the inside of him came, and he began to see the activities of God. From that time forward this broken man employed the power of the strong man's gospel by allowing the Holy Spirit to flow through him displaying the activities of God to anyone who would watch.

We must ask ourselves; "Am I allowing the Holy Spirit to flow through me, displaying to me the activities of God?" This is **key** to operating in the strong man's gospel. If you can't imagine His activities flowing through you, you will not step out and do them. Whenever God used someone in the scriptures, He had to first plant a picture in their mind of His power flowing through them. Abraham had to see a risen Isaac before offering his son. David needed to see a slain giant before he placed the stone in the sling. Esther saw herself as a favored queen before interrupting King Ahasuerus uninvited. Gideon needed to see that he was a victorious warrior before leading 300 against 135,000. Mary was required to see herself a pregnant virgin before conception took place. We must allow God to paint His pictures in our minds. Are you allowing the Holy Spirit to convince you that God has given you the gift of His mind? Paul told us in 1 Corinthians 2:16, *"For WHO HAS KNOWN THE MIND OF THE LORD, THAT HE WILL INSTRUCT HIM?* **But we have the mind of Christ**.*"*

Until we lay aside our earth-consciousness and allow the status of our noble New Birth, that of a highborn Christian, to dominate our thinking, the Holy Spirit will have difficulty revealing to us the characteristics of who we really are. He will have trouble convincing you that you are a royal child, a prince, a princess, a royal fighter. He'll have to fight to get you to see that you are one who longs to enter into a situation with everything you've got and take it captive for Jesus Christ.

You might be saying to yourself right now, "What I see, as I look around, doesn't depict nobility. My life, my circumstances reveal quite the opposite." How *do* circumstances effect this *strong man's gospel*? Men and women who get a revelation of who they really are in Christ are not overcome by the conditions they find themselves in. Instead they realize that within them lies a resource of creative power, of divine energy, the very strength of the one who birthed them. They recognize their bloodline and realize that what is flowing through their veins is supernatural. They see that they have everything they need to bring to pass the desires of His heart! **His heart** – they're broken and their own heart no longer matters! Their only desire is to demonstrate the power of God in their life.

8.

How Do We Demonstrate the Strong Man's Gospel in our Life?

There are two things you can do to demonstrate the "Strong Man's Gospel" in your life:
1. Begin to understand your union with your creator.
2. Stop crying out to God to do something, and move forward!

First, begin to understand *the mystery* of your union with your creator, the great "I am who I am!" <u>Develop</u> a consciousness of God being inside your body. Develop it! It doesn't happen overnight – Satan fights it! Say out loud, "God is inside this body!" Shout it if you have to. Do whatever it takes to *see* it! Understand that your spirit and the Spirit of the Lord Jesus Christ are one and the same. If you have joined yourself to Jesus, 1 Corinthians 6:17 tells you that you are one Spirit with Him; *"But the one who joins himself to the Lord is **<u>one spirit with Him</u>**."*

Get God-inside minded!! Every time the Holy Spirit asks you to do something, think; "God is in me," instead of, "How can I ever do that?" Get an Elijah attitude, knowing beyond a shadow of doubt that fire will come down and consume the altar no matter how much it is doused with watered down religious rhetoric. Come to **know** that there is a fire burning inside you that is just waiting to jump the fire line of natural thinking. It wants to consume your soul. You must know that it is there. Develop an awareness of this! Say out loud, "There is a fire burning inside me!" Natural thinking may contradict this, but remember, you have access to supernatural thinking; the mind of Christ!

The second thing is to stop crying out to God to do something. Move forward and begin to demonstrate the strong man's gospel in your life! You must come to understand that He has already united Himself with you and is placing His desires in your heart. He wants *you* to move forward with those desires; speaking the manifestation of them into existence by the name of Jesus Christ! Now, timing **is** an issue. It may not be *time* to see the lawyer to set up articles of incorporation! It may not be *time* to buy the travel tickets! It may not be *time* to head to Africa! It may not be *time* to build the mission, start the study, or begin the ministry! But if those desires have been planted in you by God, then it **is** time to begin speaking them into existence. In chapter 9, *What is God Waiting For?*, we will explore more about *timing* and when to *move forward*, but let's look further into how we demonstrate and give evidence to the strong man's gospel residing within.

In John's vision of the revelation of Christ we hear Jesus say, in Revelation 1:17-18, *"Do not be afraid; I am the first and the* *last, and the living One; and I was dead, and behold, **I am alive forevermore, and I have the keys of death and of Hades**.*"

How is this *"living One Who has the keys of death and Hades"* evidenced or proven today? How does the world see evidence of the Living Christ? What proof do they have that He is alive forevermore? This is only attained through you and me today! Jesus is not here on this earth today in His physical body. He is here today in the physical bodies of His brothers and sisters. This is why we are called *ambassadors* for Christ (2 Cor. 5:20). We are representing, or re-presenting Him to the world in this present year of our Lord and beyond! He presented Himself to the world 2000 years ago when He became flesh and walked among us in a body. But He, in His glorified body, *was received up into heaven, and sat down at the right hand of God* (Mk. 16:19).

Today Christ is presented to the world through the only body He has on earth, the Church. The Church, as the body of Christ, is responsible to re-present Jesus to the world this year, next year, and the one after that, until He returns. You are the only evidence of a living Christ. You and I are the evidence that He has risen, gone up, and will return just like He said.

In John 14:12-14, Jesus said; *"Truly, truly, I say to you, he who believes in Me, **the works that I do, he will do also; and greater works than these he will do**; because I go to the Father. Whatever you ask in My name, that will I do, **so that the Father may be glorified in the Son**. If you ask Me anything in My name, I will do it."* When we display Jesus' works, when we ask in His name and allow Him to "do," the Father is glorified in the Son. Get this! God is glorified in this world when we do the works of Jesus. Why? Because it proves Jesus, or gives evidence of God. When we do the works of Jesus, demonstrating the strong man's gospel, a picture or image of God is being displayed. Jesus went on to say in John 15:8, 16, *"**My Father is glorified by this, that you bear much fruit**, and so prove to be My disciples."* 16 *"You did not choose Me but I chose you, and appointed you that you would go and bear fruit, and that your fruit would remain, so that whatever you ask of the Father in My name He may give to you."*

When we bear *much fruit*, it brings glory to the Father. Now don't think of the glory as being in heaven, as in God saying, "That makes Me feel good." What Jesus is saying is that God's glory will be displayed on earth when we bear much fruit. And this *fruit* is not to be defined as godliness in moral terms. That focus is much too narrow. Listen to what John Eldredge writes about displaying God's glory on earth in *The Journey of Desire* (2000);

LITTLE GODS

"So God created man in his own image, in the image of God he created him; male and female he created them." Thus is humanity trumpeted onto the scene in verse 27 of the first chapter of Genesis (NIV). It is a passage familiar to most of us. Too familiar perhaps, for we rarely wonder about what it means. Right here, at the beginning of our existence, is the single phrase our Creator uses to characterize us, and most of us haven't the foggiest idea what it implies. If we were reading the Scripture for the story it is (and not like an encyclopedia, as many do), we would have in mind all that has transpired up to this moment. We have been watching the God whose image we bear. What do we know about him at this point? What has he been up to? Creating the heavens and the earth. Islands and caribou and wildflower. This is what he has been doing. *This is all we know of God* when we reach the point at which we are compared to him.

If you were meeting a young man for the first time, and he was introduced to you as the "son of Einstein," you'd probably expect him to be rather bright. If you met a young woman as the "daughter of Nadia Comaneci," the Russian gymnast, you might assume she could turn a decent cartwheel. We expect greatness from the offspring of the great. To be introduced as the image bearers of God is full of anticipation. It would be as though we were introduced as the sons of a renowned artist, perhaps a Monet, or as the daughters of a graceful dancer, such as Martha Graham. It leads us to what to expect next. Jesus said, "Is it not written in your Law, 'I have said you are gods'?" (John 10:34 NIV). Why is it, then, that creativity rarely comes to mind when we think of how we reflect God? More often than not we think of godliness in moral terms. When we hear that so-and-so is a "godly person," we assume that he is devout, or perhaps self-sacrificing, and certainly more virtuous than most. But when Genesis declares we are God's image, it is describing not certain qualities of our character but *capacities of our nature.* This is why, when the essence of our likeness to God is announced, it is in the context of our *position* upon earth, our place in creation:

Then God said, "Let us make man in our image, in our likeness, *and let them rule* over the fish of the sea and the birds of the air, over the livestock, over all the earth, and over all the creatures that move along the ground." (Gen. 1:26 NIV, emphasis added)

In other words, we are *made* like God in our creative powers because we are to *be* like God in ruling the earth. The image implies a capacity, and the capacity assumes the creative legacy we shall carry on. "Those two phrases – 'Let us make man in our Image,' and 'Let them rule' – must be taken together," says Ben Patterson. "Each modifies the other. To be like God is to rule the earth as he does. To rule the earth as he does is to be like God." Our original design was for a life of creative rule, to share in the overall

> care and development of God's creation. The poet writes because she is made in God's image; the builder loves to build for the same reason. Entrepreneurs risk capital venture, baseball players go to batting cages, and cooks experiment with spices all for the same reason. It is what we *are*. (p. 151-152)

We display God's glory when we rise to our *position* in Christ and become all God created us to be, ruling over that part of the earth God created each of us to rule. The fruit that remains after our time of rule will be seen in *the creative legacy we shall carry on.* God's glory is re-presented to this world generation after generation when we, as disciples, operate in our *original design* for *a life of creative rule*, and *share in the overall care and development of God's creation.* When God said, *"I said, 'You are gods, And all of you are sons of the Most High"* in Psalm 82:6, He was speaking of the *capacities of our nature* for creativity and our *position* to rule or reign in life as kings (Romans 5:17). This is the position we were originally created to occupy. Since the fall of man, this position can only be *fully* realized *"through the One, Jesus Christ"* (Romans 5:17). We are not left alone to negotiate re-entry into this position. Without a guide to take us in, re-entry would be impossible in our fallen state.

Jesus describes the Guide He provides as He continues with His instructions for demonstrating the strong man's gospel; *"But when He, the Spirit of truth, comes,* **He will guide you into all the truth**; *for He will not speak on His own initiative, but* *whatever He hears, He will speak; and* **He will disclose to you what is to come***.* **He will glorify Me, for He will take of Mine and will disclose it to you***. All things that the Father has are Mine; therefore I said that He takes of Mine and will disclose it to you"* (John 16:13-15).

When you allow the Holy Spirit to disclose to you the truth and what is to come, when you allow the Holy Spirit to take of what belongs to Jesus and give it to you, you then allow the Holy Spirit to glorify Jesus. Jesus said that all authority had been given to Him in heaven and on earth (Matthew 28:18). Jesus is glorified in this realm when we allow the Holy Spirit to *"take from Jesus and deliver to us"* (The Message) that authority to go and make disciples of all nations (vs. 19). Authority must be understood and **received** in order to authentically demonstrate the strong man's gospel. The impact of this authority can only be realized in understanding its source. Jesus describes the flow of this authority in His prayer in John 17:8-10, *"for the* **words** *which You gave Me I have given to them;* **and they received them** *and* **truly understood** *that I came forth from You, and* **they believed that You sent Me**. *I ask on their behalf; I do not ask on behalf of the world, but of those whom You have given Me; for they are Yours; and all things that are Mine are Yours, and Yours are Mine;* **and I have been glorified in them***."*

When we *receive* Jesus' words which the Father gave Him, and *truly understand* the flow of authority in demonstrating the strong man's gospel, Jesus gets glorified in us. The demonstration of the strong man's gospel on earth gives evidence of the living One, Who was dead, but is now alive forevermore

(Revelation 1:18). This flow of authority is explicitly described by Jesus a few verses later, *"**As** You sent Me into the world, **I also have sent them** into the world"* John 17:18.

In the same way Jesus represented the Father 2000 years ago, so we are to represent Him today – notice the word "**as**"!! When through *the strong man's gospel* we re-present Jesus to the world in our generation, we represent the Father to the world in the same way Jesus represented Him to His generation. The dictionary defines *"**as**"* in this way; "To the same extent or degree; equally." We act as though He said, "*With less* I have sent them into the world," or "*Worth less* I have sent them, or "*Powerless* I have sent them," because that is what religion has taught us for years. But Jesus says *as,* or "to the same extent" in which the Father sent Him, He has sent us into the world. And just in case anyone gets the mistaken idea that this was only for the disciples, or those whom are often called the "apostles," we have a clear directive from Jesus to apply this not to "these alone," but also to "those who believe in Jesus through their word." Jesus continues praying in verse 20, *"I do not ask on **behalf of these alone**, but **for those also who believe in Me through their word**."*

That is you and me! We have believed through the disciple's word! We cannot relegate this *"in the same manner"* commission to a long dead group of followers. This strong man's commission is for *everyone* who believes in Jesus through the words of Matthew, Mark, Luke and John! Now look at what Jesus astonishingly says next about the demonstration of the strong man's gospel; *"**The glory which You have given Me**"*

***I have given to them**, **that they may be one**, just as We are one"* John 17:22.

The *same* glory that was given to Jesus, He has given to us! Why? To become super-apostles? To grow large churches? So people might think well of us? So the world will know they're going to hell? No! Not at all! It is so that we might be **one** with *each other* as well as **one** with *Them*. The same glory that was flowing through Jesus has been given to us. If all of us were to release that glory, that *healing* glory, that *forgiving* glory, that *restoration* glory, that *joyful* glory, there would be no divisions among us. There would be no fighting or arguing, only doing! We would be doing! We would be doing the works that Jesus did (John 14:12). But we have neglected the glory for the sake of religion. Rather than learning to demonstrate the glory, we have chosen to argue religion's rules, and the world suffers the consequence. Jesus stated the objective of **oneness** in verse 21; *"**that they may all be one**; even as You, Father, are in Me and I in You, that they also may be in Us, **so that the world may believe** that You sent Me."*

Jesus said that the "**oneness**" would cause the world to believe that God sent Him! The problem is not with the presence of the glory, it is our neglect of its presence. Notice what Jesus prayed in verse 24; *"Father, I desire that they also, whom You have given Me, be with Me where I am, **so that they may behold My glory** which You have given Me, for You loved Me before the foundation of the world."*

We know this prayer was answered, for Paul said in Ephesians 2:6 that God, after making us alive together with Christ, *"....raised us up with Him, and seated us with Him in the heavenly places in Christ Jesus."* We are now with Him where He is! So what is the problem? The problem is *beholding*! We are not beholding His glory!

Before we define beholding, let's look at what this glory is we have been given. Vine's Expository Dictionary defines *glory* as: "used of the **nature and acts of God in self-manifestation**, i.e., **what He essentially is and does**.... (John 17:24); glory was exhibited in **the character and acts of Christ** in the days of His flesh (John 1:14, Hebrews 1:3)." According to Vine's definition, what we have been given is a supernatural, divine ability or power to walk as one with the Father, even as Jesus did! We are told in John 17 that He gave us this glory, this power, to walk in unity! Apparently unity does not come through programs, seminars, unity days, or even exhortation! It comes through the glory and the glory is only released by beholding it! How do we behold it?

Vine's definition of *behold* is: "a spectator, is used of one who looks at a thing with interest and for a purpose, usually indicating the careful observation of details."

Vine's gives examples of how the word for *behold* was translated elsewhere;

> **Look**: *looking on* (Mark 15:40)
> **Perceive:** *to be a spectator of, look at, discern; is translated perceive in John 4:19 indicating the woman's **earnest contemplation** of the Lord*
> **See:** *it points especially to the **action of the person beholding***

From these definitions we can see that *to behold* is to be a spectator of, with earnest contemplation, paying attention with careful observation of details. We have been raised up with Christ in order to carefully observe Jesus' glory, which is in us, so we may release this glory, resulting in the *oneness* Jesus described in verse 21. This unity, with each other and the Godhead, brings manifestation to the Living One who holds the keys to death and Hades, in *this* year of our Lord and beyond! This manifestation of the Living One is designed for this purpose, Jesus declared in His prayer; **"so that the world may believe that You sent Me."** When we *behold His glory* and thereby *experience oneness*, we *manifest Jesus*, giving *evidence* to the world by which they may believe that God sent Him. Understanding our union with our creator and with each other is how we begin to demonstrate and give evidence to the strong man's gospel.

9.

What is God Waiting For?

Let's go back to the statement we made earlier, "**God has already united Himself with you and is placing His desires in your heart and now expects you to move forward with those desires, speaking the manifestation of them into existence by the name of Jesus.**" Today, consultants call this "forward thinking," as though it is something the experts came up with. Well, it is *really* something "The Expert" disclosed to us many years ago when He spoke to Moses in Exodus 14:13-18. As you read these verses ask yourself this question, "What is our "forward thinking" God waiting for?"

Exodus 14:
13 *"But Moses said to the people, 'Do not fear!* **Stand by** *and see the salvation of the LORD which He will accomplish for you today; for the Egyptians whom you have seen today, you will never see them again forever.*
14 **The LORD will fight for you while you keep silent**.*'"*

In verses 13-14 Moses is telling the people to stand still, keep silent, and watch what God would do. That sounds very familiar to much religious philosophy today, doesn't it? It sounds spiritual. Moses was very much in line with the religious cliché, "Let go and let God!" But what does our forward thinking God say to Moses in verse 15? 15 *"Then the LORD said to Moses, 'Why are you crying out to **Me**? Tell **the sons of Israel** to go forward.'"*

Why are you crying out to Me, He asks? Why are you begging Me to do something? Why did you tell the sons of Israel to stand idly by? Wrong instructions Moses, my boy!! Tell the sons of Israel to go "forward"! Tell them to make their move! And then look what He tells Moses in verse 16; *"**As for you**, lift up your staff and stretch out your hand over the sea and divide it, and the sons of Israel shall go through the midst of the sea on dry land."* "As for you, Moses, quit this begging and crying out to me, **you** do something! Lift up your staff! You remember what that is, don't you Moses? It's My Power!! It's My Power!"

Let's go back and look at a little history. In Exodus 4 we find God demonstrating Himself to Moses in preparation for his leadership role. In verse 2 we read; *"The LORD said to him, 'What is that in your hand?' And he said, '**A staff**.'"* This was a shepherd's staff, the tool of Moses' trade. It was to Moses what a toolbox is to a mechanic, a scissors and comb to a barber, a Bible to a preacher, a violin to a musician. It was his livelihood! It was his life!

In verse 3 God says to Moses, *"'**Throw it on the ground**.' So he threw it on the ground, and it became a serpent; and Moses fled from it."* God told Moses to take his livelihood, his life, and lay it down. This is an important step toward brokenness. If we are unwilling to lay our life down before God we will never operate authentically in the strong man's gospel. But it is very interesting what God does with our life when we do lay it down!

God continues His instructional demonstration in verse 4; *"But the LORD said to Moses, 'Stretch out your hand and **grasp it by its tail**'—so he stretched out his hand and caught it, **and it became a staff in his hand—"*** God had Moses grasp this serpent by its tail!! Who is in control with a *tail grasp* on a snake, the snake or the man? It is definitely not the one who grasps it! The control lies in the power of the snake to turn and bite the hand that grasps it. After laying down our life before God, He will always have us pick it right back up, but only by its tail. He does not want *us* to be in control of our life. He wants us to be yielded to Him. It will no longer be us who will be in control of our life, but the power He infuses will direct us.

In throwing down his livelihood, Moses experienced the resulting power of God in his life. Something was now very different. In Exodus 4:17 God tells Moses, *"You shall take in your hand **this staff**, with which you shall perform the signs."* Then in verse 20 we read, *"So Moses took his wife and his sons and mounted them on a donkey, and returned to the land of Egypt. Moses also took **the staff of God** in his hand."*

The *"thrown down"* staff had become the *"power of God"* in Moses' life!

His staff was simply a stick until he turned it over to the Lord. When the Lord gave it back, it had become the power of God! When we give our lives, our bodies, to the Lord, they are nothing more than a stick. Our lives are simply a stick when we throw them down to Him. But when He gives them back to us, they are no longer just a stick, but the very power of God!

Moses' staff had become the power of God. And God says to him, "Lift it up, and use it! Remember what it is. It's My power, Moses! And it's in your hands, boy! Take it and use it! *You* stretch out *your* hand over the sea and divide it! When you move forward, and take the power I have given to you and use it, then the sons of Israel shall go through the midst of the sea on dry land (Ex. 14:16)." This, God said to a man who didn't have a fraction of the revelation and power we have been given. In Matthew 11:11 Jesus said, *"Truly I say to you, among those born of women there has not arisen anyone greater than John the Baptist! Yet* **the one who is least** *in the kingdom of heaven* **is greater** *than he."*

Jesus informs us that even though John the Baptist was greater than Moses, the very *least* one of us in our high-born position of sons and daughters of God under the New Covenant is greater than John the Baptist! The revelation and power Moses had access to was far inferior to what we have, and yet God rebukes him for crying out to Him! Moses had told the sons of Israel to stand still. He then went to God begging Him to do something. And God replies to Moses, "Why are you crying out to me? Move! I've given you a job. I've placed upon you a responsibility." Then in Exodus 14:16 God gives Moses the details of that responsibility, *"**And as for you** (your* job, your responsibility), *lift up your staff and stretch out your hand over the sea and divide it, and the sons of Israel shall go through the midst of the sea on dry land."*

God continues in verses 17 and 18 declaring what His own responsibility is, "**As for Me**, *behold, I will harden the hearts of the Egyptians so that they will go in after them; and I will be honored through Pharaoh and all his army, through his chariots and his horsemen. Then the Egyptians will know that I am the LORD, when I am honored through Pharaoh, through his chariots and his horsemen."* Do you see this? It was Moses' responsibility to part the sea. It was his responsibility to use God's power. And what was God's responsibility? To harden the hearts of the Egyptians! If this was the division of power under the lesser covenant enacted on lesser promises, how much more is the division of responsibility amplified under the new and greater covenant we have now?

We must understand and get a vision of the *mystery* Paul revealed in Colossians 1:27, that is, "*Christ* **in you**, *the hope of Glory."* We must grasp, not the *concept*, but the *revelation* of our complete union with the living God through which we take possession of the power of God to apply to our own needs and the needs of others. It behooves us to pursue a vision of our triumphant Christ, who says to us, *"I am the living one. I was dead, and behold I am alive forevermore and I hold the keys of death and Hades."*

But the revelation of this mystery is only to be grasped authentically with humility and in brokenness. Look at our example, Moses, in Numbers 11:17, and 25-29; *"Then I will come down and speak with you there, and I will take of the*

Spirit who is upon you, and will put Him upon them; and they shall bear the burden of the people with you, so that you will not bear it all alone......... Then the LORD came down in the cloud and spoke to him; and He took of the Spirit who was upon him and placed Him upon the seventy elders. And when the Spirit rested upon them, they prophesied. But they did not do it again. But two men had remained in the camp; the name of one was Eldad and the name of the other Medad. And the Spirit rested upon them (now they were among those who had been registered, but had not gone out to the tent), and they prophesied in the camp. So a young man ran and told Moses and said, "Eldad and Medad are prophesying in the camp." Then Joshua the son of Nun, the attendant of Moses from his youth, said, "Moses, my lord, restrain them." But Moses said to him, **"Are you jealous for my sake? Would that all the LORD'S people were prophets, that the LORD would put His Spirit upon them!"** Moses, in this event, exemplifies a <u>broken man</u> who has grasped the *strong man's gospel*. He was unconcerned that the Spirit of God might place the "spotlight" on another man. His desire was that God's Spirit shine on *all* of the Lord's people!

In Numbers 12:1-3, we see this broken man in operation during a jealous gripe session orchestrated by his sister and brother; *"Then Miriam and Aaron spoke against Moses because of the Cushite woman whom he had married (for he had married a Cushite woman); and they said, 'Has the LORD indeed spoken only through Moses? Has He not spoken through us as well?'* **And the LORD heard it**. (He hears our gripe sessions!) *Now the man Moses* **was very humble**, *more than any man who was on the face of the earth."* This humble broken man does not retaliate but simply allows the Lord to answer. And He does! In verses 5-8 God declares Moses a faithful servant with whom He speaks openly, *mouth to mouth*. God then asks Miriam and Aaron why they were unafraid to speak against Moses. Miriam becomes *leprous, as white as snow*.

How does a leader of the magnitude of Moses respond when his authority has been questioned? An unbroken man would tell Miriam that she had it coming! But this humble broken man who understood the strong man's gospel responded quite different. He prayed for her. *"O God, heal her, I pray!"* he said in verse 13. A broken man allows *the Lord* to answer those who grumble against him, and then prays for them. Moses sought no revenge against them. Now one might argue, "Well they were his sister and brother!" Well, let's look at another incident in Numbers 16:1-3;

"Now Korah the son of Izhar, the son of Kohath, the son of Levi, with Dathan and Abiram, the sons of Eliab, and On the son of Peleth, sons of Reuben, took action,

*and they rose up before Moses, together with some of the sons of Israel, two hundred and fifty leaders of the congregation, chosen in the assembly, men of renown. They assembled together against Moses and Aaron, and said to them, '****You have gone far enough, for all the congregation are holy, every one of them, and the LORD is in their midst; so why do you exalt yourselves above the assembly of the LORD****?'"*

What these 250 leaders were saying was, "Moses, you're too much of a big shot! Who set you up as a leader over us?" What does Moses do when he hears this criticism? Does he explain how God called him to this position? Does he tell them of all his exploits in the presence of Pharaoh? Does he remind them of all the miracles performed at his hand? No! Verse 4 tells us, *"When Moses heard this,* **he fell on his face***."*

> **A broken man falls on his face in the face of criticism!**

Moses fell on his face. No retribution, no retaliation. And this response came from a man who God set up as the highest authority. In Exodus 4:15-16 we hear God say to Moses, *"You are to speak to him (Aaron) and put the words in his mouth; and I, even I, will be with your mouth and his mouth, and I will teach you what you are to do. Moreover, he shall speak for you to the people; and he will be as a mouth for you and* **you will be as God to him***."*

"You will be as God to him!!" Moses was a man who God could trust with His power, because he was a broken man, a humble servant leader!

A broken man is a man God can trust with His power!

God is waiting for men and women of brokenness to move forward in the power of the strong man's gospel.

10.

How do we take possession of the power of God?

If God is waiting for *us* to move forward in the power of the strong man's gospel, what is it we must do to take possession of the power within it? Let's look in Mark 5:25-34 to see how someone did; *"A woman who had had a hemorrhage for twelve years, and had endured much at the hands of many physicians, and had spent all that she had and was not helped at all, but rather had grown worse — after hearing about Jesus, she came up in the crowd behind Him and touched His cloak. For she thought, '**If I just touch His garments, I will get well**.' Immediately the flow of her blood was dried up; and she felt in her body that she was healed of her affliction.*

*Immediately Jesus, **perceiving in Himself that the power proceeding from Him had gone forth**, turned around in the crowd and said, 'Who touched My garments?' And His disciples said to Him, "**You see the crowd pressing in on You**, and You say, 'Who touched Me?'" And He looked around to see the woman who had done this. But the woman fearing and* trembling, aware of what had happened to her, came and fell down before Him and told Him the whole truth. And He said to her, '**Daughter, your faith has made you well**; go in peace and be healed of your affliction.'"

This woman took possession of the power of God by adopting an attitude that declared, "I'm going to press through! I'm going to press through this crowd, this criticism, this failure, this depression, this fear, and I'm going to extract power from the Messiah! I'm not going to let anyone or anything get in my way! I'm reaching in and grabbing hold of what He's got!" This woman was determined.

Let's explore this a little deeper by examining what this scenario of Jesus and this woman shows us about God's ways. Now doesn't it seem that if God was reasonable, He'd have told Jesus, "Hey Son, there's a lady on the outside of this crowd who needs your attention. Go out and touch her"? But this isn't God's way. He requires us to "press in" to extract or *place a draw* on His power. He wants us to place a demand on His power.

> **God wants us to place a demand on His power**

In Luke 18:2-8 Jesus likened this "pressing in" to a widow who kept coming to an unrighteous judge, "placing a demand" on him until she extracted power. Let's take a look at this parable;

"*In a certain city there was a judge who did not fear God and did not respect man. There was a widow in that city, **and*** *she kept coming to him, saying, 'Give me legal protection from my opponent.' For a while he was unwilling; but afterward he said to himself, 'Even though I do not fear God nor respect man, yet because this widow bothers me, I will give her legal protection, otherwise by continually coming she will wear me out.' And the Lord said, 'Hear what the unrighteous judge said; now,* **will not God bring about justice for His elect** *who cry to Him day and night, and will He delay long over them?* **I tell you that He will bring about justice for them quickly. However, when the Son of Man comes, will He find faith on the earth**?'"

Going back to verse 1, we read, *"Now He was telling them a parable to show that* **at all times <u>they</u> ought to pray and not to lose heart**.*"* In this we see that Jesus was **showing** them that *"at all times they ought to pray and not to lose heart."* He is not talking about *begging* God, but rather *placing a demand* on and *standing on* His power and authority. His point here is **the woman, not the judge**! This judge is not like God in any way. He clearly shows this in verse 2; *"...there was a judge* <u>**who did not fear God and did not respect man,**</u>*"* and verse 6, *"...the Lord said, 'Hear what the* <u>**unrighteous judge**</u> *said.'"* This parable is *not* a comparison to God! In fact, God is so much unlike this judge that Jesus says in verses 7-8, *"now, will not God bring about justice for His elect who cry to Him day and night, and will He delay long over them? I tell you that He will bring about justice for them quickly.* **However**, *when the Son of Man comes,* <u>**will He find faith on the earth**</u>?"

The **woman and her faith** is the issue in this text, not God's willingness!!

The question that needs to be answered then is not one of *God's* willingness, but rather, one of *our* willingness! Are *we* willing to press in, use our faith, actually reach out with the demand of faith, which God honors, and draw on His power? Jesus' point here is that we cannot have an attitude of, "Whatever God wants." No! **Will He find faith?** Will there be any supernatural faith that refuses defeat, supernatural faith that sees victory, supernatural faith that believes God hears and answers when there is no physical evidence of it?

Looking at the experiences of this widow and the woman with the issue of blood, what was the worst that could happen to them? *Nothing*!! Isn't that right? With all of their pressing in, the worst that could happen to them is that *nothing* be accomplished. So what did they have to lose? **Nothing**! What is happening with most Christians today? *Nothing*! So what have they got to lose by pressing in and believing God for something? **Nothing**! Here is where we miss it. We think we'll lose our reputation, when the truth is we shouldn't have one. We're so afraid of failure; "What if it doesn't work? What if nothing happens?" Those are silly thoughts, for *nothing* will happen anyway!! So what is there to lose? Our ministry? Our church? That is what we fear, losing our spiritual credibility!!

If we call on the power of God, if we press in and place a demand on the authority we've been given and nothing happens, we fear we will no longer be credible. But if we expect *nothing* and *nothing* happens we somehow expect to remain credible. Wow!!! What do we have to lose, really? *Nothing*! What do we have to gain? Possession of the power of God! Most Christians are waiting for God to tell Jesus to "go outside

How do we take possession of the power of God?

---

the crowd," but that is not God's way! He requires us to press in and "grab hold of" His power! Look at what Jesus told the woman with the issue of blood in Mark 5:34; *"And He said to her, 'Daughter, **your faith has made you well**; go in peace and be healed of your affliction.'"*

*"**Your** faith has made you well."* He gave her the credit!! Do you see that? We miss this with our wimpy "don't tell me I don't have enough faith" attitude. Now we know it isn't our "human, drum it up in the flesh, I'm gonna believe this faith thing" kind of faith that accomplishes anything. But when we decide to appropriate His faith which He birthed in us, things happen. We are told in 1 John 5:4, *"For whatever is **born of God** overcomes the world; and **this** is the victory that has overcome the world—**our faith**."* **Our faith is birthed of God!** Our faith is birthed of God and when we appropriate it, John tells us the world is overcome. And then, God gives us the credit for using His faith! That is so *Him*, to be this generous!

Our faith is birthed of God!

From these examples illustrating taking possession of the power of God, we find there are two requirements for taking possession of this power. The first is expectation. ***Expectation!!!*** Both of these women *expected* something and both were willing to "do whatever it took" to receive it. That is what Jesus was saying in the parable, "Make your expectation so strong that you refuse to accept any hindrance that the devil throws your way." The devil is the one who gets in the way.

This was revealed to Daniel at a time when he was "pressing in" to draw on the power of God. After three weeks of prayer an angel appears to him and informs him of the delay. In Daniel 10:2-3, 12-14 we read; "*In those days, I, Daniel, had been mourning for **three entire weeks**. I did not eat any tasty food, nor did meat or wine enter my mouth, nor did I use any ointment at all until the entire three weeks were completed....... Then he said to me, "Do not be afraid, Daniel, for **from the first day that you set your heart on understanding this and on humbling yourself before your God**, your words were heard, and I have come in response to your words. But the **prince** of the kingdom of Persia **was withstanding me for twenty-one days**; then behold, Michael, one of the chief princes, came to help me, for I had been left there with the kings of Persia. Now I have come to give you an understanding of what will happen to your people in the latter days, for the vision pertains to the days yet future.""* For three weeks the devil held back God's response to Daniel!

Satan does everything he can to halt the flow of God's power from breaking through into the physical dimension. God does not withhold His power from us like the unrighteous judge in Jesus' parable. Rather He has already extended it toward us who believe, as we are told in Ephesians 1:19. In Jesus' parable of the widow He is telling us to refuse to take no for an answer from the devil! And the woman with the issue of blood; what was her hindrance? Besides the pressing crowd, the very illness itself was a hindrance. She was unclean and had no business being near a crowd, let alone "pressing" her way through it! Why did she do it? Expectation! She expected the crowd," but that is not God's way! He requires us to press in and "grab hold of" His power! Look at what Jesus told the woman with the issue of blood in Mark 5:34; *"And He said to her, 'Daughter, **your faith has made you well**; go in peace and be healed of your affliction.'"*

*"**Your** faith has made you well."* He gave her the credit!! Do you see that? We miss this with our wimpy "don't tell me I don't have enough faith" attitude. Now we know it isn't our "human, drum it up in the flesh, I'm gonna believe this faith thing" kind of faith that accomplishes anything. But when we decide to appropriate His faith which He birthed in us, things happen. We are told in 1 John 5:4, *"For whatever is **born of God** overcomes the world; and **this** is the victory that has overcome the world—**our faith**."* **Our faith is birthed of God!** Our faith is birthed of God and when we appropriate it, John tells us the world is overcome. And then, God gives us the credit for using His faith! That is so *Him*, to be this generous!

> **Our faith is birthed of God!**

From these examples illustrating taking possession of the power of God, we find there are two requirements for taking possession of this power. The first is expectation. ***Expectation!!!*** Both of these women *expected* something and both were willing to "do whatever it took" to receive it. That is what Jesus was saying in the parable, "Make your expectation so strong that you refuse to accept any hindrance that the devil throws your way." The devil is the one who gets in the way.

This was revealed to Daniel at a time when he was "pressing in" to draw on the power of God. After three weeks of prayer an angel appears to him and informs him of the delay. In Daniel 10:2-3, 12-14 we read; "*In those days, I, Daniel, had been mourning for* **three entire weeks.** *I did not eat any tasty food, nor did meat or wine enter my mouth, nor did I use any ointment at all until the entire three weeks were completed……. Then he said to me, "Do not be afraid, Daniel, for* **from the first day that you set your heart on understanding this and on humbling yourself before your God**, *your words were heard, and I have come in response to your words. But the* **prince** *of the kingdom of Persia* **was withstanding me for twenty-one days**; *then behold, Michael, one of the chief princes, came to help me, for I had been left there with the kings of Persia. Now I have come to give you an understanding of what will happen to your people in the latter days, for the vision pertains to the days yet future.""* For three weeks the devil held back God's response to Daniel!

Satan does everything he can to halt the flow of God's power from breaking through into the physical dimension. God does not withhold His power from us like the unrighteous judge in Jesus' parable. Rather He has already extended it toward us who believe, as we are told in Ephesians 1:19. In Jesus' parable of the widow He is telling us to refuse to take no for an answer from the devil! And the woman with the issue of blood; what was her hindrance? Besides the pressing crowd, the very illness itself was a hindrance. She was unclean and had no business being near a crowd, let alone "pressing" her way through it! Why did she do it? Expectation! She expected results. Who was going to accuse her once she got in there and got her miracle? It wouldn't matter then!

That takes us to the second requirement revealed in these examples, that is, eliminate unworthiness. **Eliminate unworthiness!!** This woman had to shake off all sense of unworthiness in order to "mingle" with the crowd of well folks. The religious hierarchy of her day had convinced her that it was because of her sin that she was in the condition she was. She would have had to eradicate this "sin consciousness" before she could find the courage to press through the crowd and touch the cloak of the Messiah. If we expect to go in and place a demand on the power of God, we too must eradicate the "sin consciousness" that so many of us deal with. Look at the widow in Jesus' parable. She could have said, "Who am I? I'm just a *nobody*." But she didn't. She kept pressing in, ignoring the social differences, and confidently drew on the judge's power. Notice her persistence in Luke 18:3, *"There was a widow in that city, and she **kept coming to him**, saying, '**Give me legal protection** from my opponent.'"*

She wanted legal protection. She knew what was hers. She knew her rights and was unwilling to settle for less. Now someone might respond, "You can't go into God's presence acting like your worthy, that's blasphemous." There is no other way to get into God's presence but *by* worthiness! But it's not our worthiness that gets us in there. It is Jesus' worthiness. Many people think you can't go into God's presence worthily, that you cannot approach with the mindset that you are worthy of an audience. What are they thinking? Your failure is not going to grant you an audience with the Almighty. You've *got* to enter worthily, but your only hope of worthiness is Jesus. That is the legal right we are talking about! That is the legal protection from "our opponent" we are demanding!

Even if God, in your unworthiness, could grant you audience, would He want to? Think about it. He is in relationship with you. Just like you are in relationship with your mate, He is in relationship with you. Now, what if you'd greet your mate with one of those "I'm so unworthy, I'm such a failure" routines that you give God. How would that make your mate feel? Would they say "Yep, that's why I married you"? Of course not! That doesn't edify your mate and neither does coming to God with that attitude edify Him! He's the King of kings, not the King of failures. He's the Lord of lords, not the Lord of unworthy peasants. No, we come in with a worthiness attitude, and say, "Thank you Lord that the price has been paid. Thank you for making me a joint heir with Jesus. Thank you that everything has been freely given to me with Him. I'm coming in here expecting and I'm coming in here worthy of receiving because I'm here by the Blood of the Lamb." He'll give you what you need!! He'll give you what you need to draw on His power.

Another widow in the Bible called out to God and was given what she needed to draw on His power. In 2 Kings 4:1-6 we find her story. *"Now a certain woman of the wives of the sons of the prophets cried out to Elisha, 'Your servant my husband is dead, and you know that your servant feared the LORD; and the creditor has come to take my two children to be his slaves.' Elisha said to her, 'What shall I do for you?* **Tell me, what do you have in the house**?*' And she said, 'Your maidservant has nothing in the house except a jar of oil.' Then he said,* **'Go,**

borrow vessels at large for yourself from all your neighbors, even empty vessels; do not get a few. *And you shall go in and shut the door behind you and your sons, and pour out into all these vessels, and you shall set aside what is full.' So she went from him and shut the door behind her and her sons; they were bringing the vessels to her and she poured. When the vessels were full, she said to her son, 'Bring me another vessel.' And he said to her,* ***'There is not one vessel more.' And the oil stopped***.*"*

Elisha didn't give her anything!! He didn't *come* to give her anything. He said, "What do <u>you</u> have?" She answered, "Nothing but this." And Elisha said, "Use it!" She was stagnant, doing nothing! So Elisha simply moved her from stagnation to action. He told her to find an outlet, a channel through which what she had could flow. "Borrow vessels!" he said. She had everything she needed right there in the house, she just didn't have an outlet for it!! She was stuck, stagnant, paralyzed by fear; "I'm going to lose my children!" Elisha didn't tell her, "The Red Cross will be here tomorrow." He just released her from the paralysis that the fear produced. He did it by showing her what she had, not giving her what she thought she needed.

This is exactly the way it is with us and our needs. We go to God and He says, "What do you have?" This is where a little knowledge *helps*. We need to make sure we know what we have. We can then say, "All I have is this gift, and this one, and I kind of have a little enthusiasm, but that's about all." He then tells us, "Go gather vessels. Find an outlet." We just need to use what we have, by getting our minds off of ourselves and pouring what we do have into other vessels, believing that God is going to multiply the supply because of our demand of faith on His power! I am convinced that every time I go begging God, He tells me, "You have something you are not using!"

I'd like to be your Elisha today, and come, not to meet your need, but to ask you, "What do you have?" When you tell me what you have, I'd then tell you "Go gather vessels!" This widow kept pouring, it says in verse 6, until she ran out of vessels. Your supply won't stop until there is "not one vessel more."

11.

How Do We Prevent the Marking Off of Boundaries?

Have you ever wondered why we don't see more manifestation of God's glory than what we do? The Israelite's wilderness experience gives us insight into one of the reasons. In Psalm 78:42 we read this about the Israelites; *"They **did not remember** His power, The day when He redeemed them from the adversary."* Now let's go back and read verses 40-41; *"How often they **rebelled against Him** in the wilderness And **grieved Him** in the desert! Again and again they tempted God, And **pained** the Holy One of Israel."* The NIV translation reads, *"....they **vexed** the Holy One of Israel."*

The Israelites rebelled against God in the wilderness. How? By not remembering His power! And what did not remembering His power do? Verse 41 says that it tempted God and vexed, or *limited* Him. The KJV translation actually uses the word *limited*. The Israelites "vexed" God. To vex means to disturb, annoy or irritate. But the Hebrew word that was translated, *pained, vexed,* and *limited,* actually means "to mark off," as in "to mark out the boundaries of a place." What did God want to do for the Israelites? He wanted to take them all the way into the Promised Land! But they limited His intervention on their behalf. The Living Bible puts it this way, *"they…..limited the Holy One of Israel from giving them his blessings."*

The people marked off the boundaries limiting Him from displaying His power in their lives. They said, "We'd rather die in the wilderness than go into the Promised Land" (see Numbers 13 & 14 [14:2]) He could do no more for them than what they were willing to believe Him for, and they could not believe Him for much because they had forgotten His power. They neglected to look back on His miraculous deliverances and use those memories to catapult them into faith. This same "marking off of boundaries" is expressed in Jeremiah 29:11 where God expresses with great pathos His true desire for a people who had just become Babylonian slaves by their own choice. God shares with them that this was not His desire in any way, shape, or form. He says, *"For I **know** the plans that I have for you, plans for welfare and not for calamity to give you a future and a hope."*

The Israelites had forgotten God's power and they had forgotten Him. When we forget God's power, we forget Him. When we forget Him, we limit Him. When we limit Him, we will not see the oil multiplied in our lives. In fact, when we limit Him, we don't even *see* the oil that we have. We need Elishas to come and shake us out of our fear and self-centeredness. We need Elishas to remind us of the day He redeemed us from the adversary. We need Elishas to ask us, "What do you

11.

How Do We Prevent the Marking Off of Boundaries?

Have you ever wondered why we don't see more manifestation of God's glory than what we do? The Israelite's wilderness experience gives us insight into one of the reasons. In Psalm 78:42 we read this about the Israelites; *"They **did not remember** His power, The day when He redeemed them from the adversary."* Now let's go back and read verses 40-41; *"How often they **rebelled against Him** in the wilderness And **grieved Him** in the desert! Again and again they tempted God, And **pained** the Holy One of Israel."* The NIV translation reads, *"....they **vexed** the Holy One of Israel."*

The Israelites rebelled against God in the wilderness. How? By not remembering His power! And what did not remembering His power do? Verse 41 says that it tempted God and vexed, or *limited* Him. The KJV translation actually uses the word *limited*. The Israelites "vexed" God. To vex means to disturb, annoy or irritate. But the Hebrew word that was translated, *pained, vexed,* and *limited,* actually means "to mark off," as in "to mark out the boundaries of a place." What did God want to do for the Israelites? He wanted to take them all the way into the Promised Land! But they limited His intervention on their behalf. The Living Bible puts it this way, *"they.....limited the Holy One of Israel from giving them his blessings."*

The people marked off the boundaries limiting Him from displaying His power in their lives. They said, "We'd rather die in the wilderness than go into the Promised Land" (see Numbers 13 & 14 [14:2]) He could do no more for them than what they were willing to believe Him for, and they could not believe Him for much because they had forgotten His power. They neglected to look back on His miraculous deliverances and use those memories to catapult them into faith. This same "marking off of boundaries" is expressed in Jeremiah 29:11 where God expresses with great pathos His true desire for a people who had just become Babylonian slaves by their own choice. God shares with them that this was not His desire in any way, shape, or form. He says, *"For I **know** the plans that I have for you, plans for welfare and not for calamity to give you a future and a hope."*

The Israelites had forgotten God's power and they had forgotten Him. When we forget God's power, we forget Him. When we forget Him, we limit Him. When we limit Him, we will not see the oil multiplied in our lives. In fact, when we limit Him, we don't even *see* the oil that we have. We need Elishas to come and shake us out of our fear and self-centeredness. We need Elishas to remind us of the day He redeemed us from the adversary. We need Elishas to ask us, "What do you have?" We need Elishas to tell us to rise up out of our fear and paralysis and begin to "reign in life." We need Elishas who will explain to us the meaning behind what God revealed in Romans 5:17; *"For if by the transgression of the one, death reigned through the one, much more those who receive the abundance of grace and of the gift of righteousness **will reign in life** through the One, Jesus Christ."*

God said that *those who receive the abundance of grace and of the gift of righteousness **will reign in life** through the One, Jesus Christ.* To reign means to "hold sway; prevail or predominate." In this context it means "to live the high life" of God in this life. How do we do this? How do we live the high life of God in this life? We do it by exalting God's Word. We can *reign* in this life if we are resolved to enter the *high life of God*, if we are resolved to enter into a consciousness of heavenly dominion as a *world overcomer*.

We can reign in this life if we exalt God's Word. But in order to do that, we really need to learn what it means to exalt. To exalt means to glorify or to honor. When we exalt God's Word we place a higher value on it than on anything else. We let *it* move us more than anything else we experience!

Exalting God's Word is more than *knowing* God's Word. There is a very big difference between knowing God's Word and allowing God's Word to *move you*. Many people know the Word of God, but few allow it to move them more than what they see or feel. They have not elevated it to a place where they say; "This is God's Word for me!" Their faith is not based on what God said, but on what men on earth are telling them.

> **There is a very big difference between knowing God's Word and allowing God's Word to move you.**

Your faith must be based on His Word! You must exalt it to a higher place than anything else including prophecy, dreams, visions, even an audible voice. It must be esteemed more than the word of your teacher, your pastor, your mother, your father, or your mentor. How do you know when you have esteemed it to that level? Well, you have to ask yourself, what are you more moved by, what God said, or the doctor, the lawyer, the banker? Do you get upset by one word from one of these men when you have thousands of Words from God regarding the same subject? What controls you?

If we want to enter into a consciousness of heavenly dominion we must esteem the Word higher than the natural realm. Paul instructs us how to do this in Colossians 3:1-2, *"Therefore if you have been raised up with Christ, **keep seeking the things above**, where Christ is, seated at the right hand of God. **Set your mind on the things above, not on the things that are on earth**."*

He tells us to set our minds on the things above, not on the things in the natural realm! "Keep seeking and thinking on things in the spiritual realm, not the natural realm," he said. Do you remember what natural realm thinking does? It creates a fire line that must then be jumped by the Holy Spirit's fire. You must let the Word of God move you, control you, reducing the width of that natural thinking fire line! It is not *how much you know* but *how much what you do know, affects you*! You can get more mileage from allowing one verse to *affect* you than from simply *knowing* 20,000 verses. Let a verse like James 1:5, Hebrews 1:3 or John 3:16 affect you, and then share it with someone else. We are told in 2 Timothy 3:16 that *"**All** scripture is inspired by God and profitable for teaching…"* One verse is inspired! One verse contains all the power you need to reign in life!! Hebrews 4:12 tells us that the Word of God is living. It is alive and active. It will activate your soul if you will allow it to spill over from the spirit realm into the realm of your mind, will and emotions. When you allow God's Word to affect you in this way, it will prevent you from marking off the boundaries and limiting the Holy One of Israel from giving you His blessings.

12.

What's in a Name, Anyway?

So often we look for confirmation of God's Word through our natural realm senses. The fact that God *said it* is *not* good enough for us! When we were little, many of us sang a Sunday school song that went like this; "God said it, I believe it, and that settles it for me!" But as we grew older we somehow became **unsettled** with this kind of faith. We began to adopt adult sentiments such as "I'll believe it when I *see* it" as a litmus test to determine whether or not something was so. Spiritual sensitivities lost their strength as we began to depend more and more upon our physical senses.

As adults we neglect the fact that Jesus told us many times that we have two sets of eyes and two sets of ears. Numerous times He said, *"He who has ears to hear, let him hear"* – Mark 4:23, 7:16. In Mark 8:18 He asked, *"Having eyes, do you not see, and having ears do you not hear?"* He told Thomas, who boldly declared he was completely dependent on his physical senses, *"Blessed are those who did not see and yet believed"-* John 20:25, 29. Paul tells us we are to look at things that are *not seen* rather than things that *are seen* – 2 Corinthians 4:18. We must use something other than our *sense eyes* to see unseen (eternal, spiritual) things. According to Hebrews 11:1, faith is what we use to do this. The Amplified version puts it this way, *"faith perceiving as real fact what is not revealed to the senses."* James tells us we have two tongues, one inspired by the natural realm and one by the spiritual – James 3:8-10. Paul tells us we have the mind of Christ but also recognizes the reality and influence of the natural mind.

It is not that we are to ignore our natural realm senses but we are not to allow them to rule us. Our natural senses give us information about the natural realm. They give us information about *facts*. Paul says these natural realm *facts* are subject to change. They are only temporal. That is why we are to place a lesser value on those things than what we see, hear, taste, smell and feel with our *spiritual senses*. The information derived from these senses is eternal. That is why the Word of God calls this information truth and informs us that eternal, unchanging *truth* always supersedes temporal, changing *facts*.

The purpose of our natural senses is that we might enjoy the natural realm we live in. But if we want to *influence* this 'temporal' realm with the truth of the eternal realm, we must subjugate the feelings of the natural realm to those of the spiritual. Paul, in Romans 8:6, reveals the consequences of doing otherwise. He says, *"For the mind set on* (established only in) *the flesh* (natural senses) *is death* (facts will rule), *but the mind set on the Spirit is life and peace."* If our minds are established only in the natural senses, facts will rule and we will experience the results of those facts. On the other hand, if our minds are established in spiritual realm sensitivities, truth will prevail over the facts and produce nothing but life and peace. The only way to establish our minds *on the Spirit* is to elevate **God's Word** to the highest level of value in our life. Jesus said in John 6:63, *"...the **words** that I have spoken to you are **spirit** and are **life**."*

> **If we want to influence the natural realm with the truth of the eternal realm, we must subjugate the feelings of the natural realm to those of the spiritual.**

Look at what Peter says about elevating God's Word to this level. In light of his witnessing the transfiguration of Jesus, in 2 Peter 1:17-21 (AMP) he writes ; *"For when He was invested with honor and glory from God the Father and a voice was borne to Him by the [splendid] Majestic Glory [in the bright cloud that overshadowed Him, saying], This is My beloved Son in Whom I am well pleased and delight, We [actually] heard this voice borne out of heaven, for we were together with Him on the holy mountain.* **And we have the prophetic word [made] firmer still. You will do well to pay close attention to *it*** *as to a lamp shining in a dismal (squalid and dark) place, until the day breaks through [the gloom] and the Morning Star rises (comes into being) in your hearts.* (We will want to find out what the "**it**" we are to pay attention to is.) *[Yet] first [you must] understand this, that no **prophecy of Scripture** is [a matter] of any personal or private or special interpretation (loosening, solving). For no prophecy ever originated because some man willed it [to do so—it never came by human impulse], but **men***

spoke from God *who were borne along (moved and impelled) by the Holy Spirit.*

Beck's Translation of verses 19 and 20 gives us insight on what Peter was telling us to pay close attention to: *"And we have **a more sure word of prophecy**. Please look to **it** as to a light shining in a gloomy place……. Understand this first, that no one can explain any **written Word of God** as he likes….."*

Nothing supersedes the written Word of God. He informs us that he saw the transfigured Christ, saw the overshadowing cloud of God's glory, actually heard the voice of God declaring Jesus as His son, and then tells us that we have a *"more sure word of prophecy,"* that is the *"written Word of God."* A. S. Worrell, in his translation of the New Testament, comments on this "**more sure** prophetic word" in this way; "the prophetic word, as a system of revelation from God, was more calculated to carry conviction than any verbal report, such as he gave them of the transfiguration on the mount."

This elevation of God's Word over anything we might see with our natural eyes, hear with our natural ears, or feel with our natural senses in confirmed by David in Psalm 138:2. The KJV reads; *"I will worship toward thy holy temple, and praise thy name for thy lovingkindness and for thy truth: for thou hast **magnified thy word above all thy name**."* Beck's translates it this way; *"…and have made Your name and Your promise **greater than everything**."* The Amplified puts it like this; *"…for You have exalted above all else Your name and Your word and **You have magnified Your word above all Your name**!"*

This verse indicates that God has exalted His Word above everything, even His very Name. This is because God's Word is what makes His Name. If God's Word is no good, His Name would be no good. Suppose you had a friend named Frank who lied all the time. If you then told another friend something and when asked how you knew it was true, you told them Frank told you, they would laugh. Why? Because his "word" makes his name! If God's Word didn't work, His Name wouldn't work. The *Name of God* derives its power from the *Word of God*. So closely are they associated that John, speaking of the Christ, writes in Revelation 19:13, *"...and His name is called The Word of God."* You see, **nothing** supersedes His written Word.

The bottom line is this; you don't need God coming to you in a vision telling you that you are a prince, a child of the King. You don't need an angelic visitation declaring your royalty. 1 Peter 2:9 has already made declaration of your royalty. God is speaking to you about *your* royalty in Esther 4:14 where Mordacai said, *"Who knows whether you have not attained royalty for such a time as this,"* You don't need a vision about these things. He told you these things in the *"more sure Word of prophecy"* that men of old, moved by the Holy Spirit wrote down for you and me. God has staked His Name on His Word. What's in a name, anyway? Only one's word! And God says you can count on His! So move forward, lift up your staff, stretch out your hand over the sea of your life and speak dominion over it. All authority and power have been given to you to trample on serpents and scorpions and over all the power of the enemy.

In Luke 10:19 Jesus said, *"Behold, I give unto you **power to tread on serpents and scorpions, and over all the power of the enemy: and nothing shall by any means hurt you**."* God has delivered and imparted to you a strong man's gospel. He wants you to share that good news with the timid, the fearful, and the fallen, so they too may become mighty warriors in the Kingdom of God, following the Captain of our Host, Jesus. It is time (and all of us need this exhortation) to lay weak, wimpy, joyless Christianity aside and understand that we *are* the army of the Lord. It is time to pick up our weapons, listen as He utters His command, and carry out His Word as the victorious army that we are!

13.

Excuse me?

The excuses need to go! The excuses that keep us from embracing brokenness need to go. The excuses that keep us from picking up the strong man's gospel need to go.

The *self-doubt excuse* of Moses needs to go; "Who am I that I should go to Pharaoh?" "Oh my Lord, I am not eloquent," he says, while the scriptures paint a different reality. In Acts 7:22 the truth of Moses' stature and eloquence is revealed; *"Moses was **educated** in all the **learning of the Egyptians**, and he was a **man of power in <u>words</u> and deeds**."* The truth was that Moses was a man of stature and powerful in speech, educated in all the learning of the Egyptians. This means he learned to speak eloquently long before whimpering to God about being unqualified. Acts 7:22 was Moses' reality! We need to see the truth about what God's Word says about us and dispossess the *self-doubt excuse* of Moses. We need to follow his example. He rose up and took hold of the strong man's gospel and led a nation into their destiny.

The *social status excuse* needs to go. The Gideon complex must be dealt with; "Oh my Lord, how can I save Israel? Indeed my clan is the weakest in Manasseh, and I am the least in my father's house." Your social status does not impress God. He won't answer you with, "Oh you're right, I didn't realize you didn't have the right social credentials for the job." No, He says, *"Surely I will be with you and you shall defeat Midian as one man"* – Judges 6:16. We must discard the *social status excuse* and follow Gideon's example. Gideon rose up, took hold of the strong man's gospel and set Israel free from Midianite oppression.

The *minimal stature excuse* needs to go. David was left out of the lineup when Samuel came to his father's house to find the next king of Israel – 1 Samuel 16:6-12. His father didn't think this young boy who was simply a shepherd would be a candidate Samuel would want to consider. But Samuel anointed him and the Spirit of the Lord came mightily upon him – verse 13. David set aside the *minimal stature excuse* and went on to become the greatest war hero and king in Israel's history. He stood face to face with a giant named Goliath and boldly took him out in the name of the Lord with a stone and a sling.

You have been anointed in the manner of David – 1 John 2:20, 27! God expects you to set aside the *minimal stature excuse*, and with the strong man's gospel destroy the giants in your life that are keeping you from living the abundant life He came to give. David understood brokenness and the strong man's gospel, and victory characterized his life. Victory can characterize yours as well.

The *lonely-hearts excuse* needs to go. Elijah, after a very successful career as a prophet of God, succumbs to the *lonely-hearts excuse*. He joined a club that is difficult to disjoin. God finds him there and asks, *"What are you doing here, Elijah?"* – 1 Kings 19:9. Elijah answers by telling God how zealous he has been for Him and declaring, *"And I alone am left; and they seek my life to take it away"* – verse 10. God, in a still, small voice, proceeded to show Elijah that he must become *still* from doing his own works, and *small* in his own opinion – verses 11-13. Then God asks him once again, *"What are you doing here, Elijah?"* Pride continues to rule and Elijah answers God in the same way, "I've worked so hard and now I'm all alone" – verse14. Brokenness evaded Elijah and he could not break free from the lonely-hearts club and drop his excuse. So God excused Elijah and instructed him to anoint Elisha to take his place. If you find yourself weary in ministry, feeling like you alone are left, and do not allow God to pull you out of the lonely-hearts cave, He *will* excuse you and pass your 'mantle' to another. So drop the *lonely-hearts excuse*, pick up the strong man's gospel, and press on with the thousands who have not bowed the knee to Baal – verse 18!

The *big visions, shattered dreams excuse* needs to go. Peter had big plans. He and his Messiah were going to change the world. He told Jesus how it would happen – Matthew 16:22. He would defend his master to the end – Matthew 26:33. He even demonstrated his commitment by slicing off the ear of one who came to take his Lord – John 18:10. Then the whole plan came crashing down at the sound of a rooster crowing. The One he swore he would defend to the end had become the One he swore that he never knew – Matthew 26:69-75. Peter's grand vision was reduced to shattered dreams. He couldn't even stand up to a servant-girl, so he decided to go back to fishing – John 21:3. And just like his dreams, he caught nothing. But Jesus came to the beach to restore Peter's vision. He dumped 153 large fish in Peter's empty net and inspired him to swim to shore. Jesus planted a new dream in Peter's heart, the dream of a shepherd (verses 15-17), and Peter went on to bring 3000 lambs into the fold the first time he spoke – Acts 2:41. He dropped his *big visions, shattered dreams excuse*, took to heart a new dream and with the strong man's gospel turned the world upside down. When your visions turn to shattered dreams, let Jesus impart to you a new dream. Drop your excuses, and boldly move forward with the strong man's gospel.

The *not my fault excuse* needs to go. God had given the kingdom of Israel into the hands of Saul. But King Saul could not let go of the *not my fault excuse*. When he disregarded biblical ethics and offered a burnt offering himself, it was Samuel's fault, not his own that he *had* to do this – 1Samuel 13:11-12! When he failed to obey God's orders and allowed King Agag and the best sheep, oxen, and lambs to live, it was the people's fault that this happened, not his own–1 Samuel 15:9-21. Saul's *not my fault excuse* kept him from embracing brokenness and without brokenness there would be no way he could authentically embrace the strong man's gospel and lead Israel. God had to take the kingdom from Saul and give it to one who had learned to embrace both. If we want to authentically embrace the strong man's gospel we must first drop the *not my fault excuse* and embrace brokenness.

The *defeatist excuse* needs to go. Joshua experienced great victory in the heavily fortified city of Jericho then immediately experienced defeat in the relatively small city of Ai. The *defeatist excuse* caused him to blame God and nearly cost Joshua his promised land. He said to God, *"If only we had been willing to dwell beyond the Jordon"* – Joshua 7:7-9. Because of his *defeatist excuse*, Joshua was willing to settle for less than what God had promised him. He was ready to go back to the wilderness side of the river! God had to shake the *defeatist excuse* from Joshua's hands. He said, *"Rise up! Why is it that you have fallen on your face?"* – verse 10. God goes on to tell Joshua that it was not His fault that Israel experienced defeat, but that one of Israel's own, Achan by name, had broken covenant with God. He reiterates His intentions for Joshua's success and gets him to shake loose the *defeatist excuse*. Joshua then picks up the strong man's gospel once more and takes the city of Ai. When we experience defeat, we must first remember that defeat is not God's intention. We must then drop the *defeatist excuse*, rise up, stretching out the javelin of victory (Joshua 8:26), and with the strong man's gospel take the land that was promised to us through Jesus Christ.

The *childhood deprivation excuse* needs to go; "You don't know what I grew up with, what I had to endure as a child. My upbringing did not prepare me for this." Esther grew up an orphan, was raised by her cousin Mordecai, yet became a queen and took hold of the strong man's gospel. After Mordecai challenged her *childhood deprivation excuse* saying,

"Who knows whether you have not attained royalty for such a time as this?" she moved forward – Esther 4:14! In the face of potential death, she boldly approached her king un-summoned, and delivered her people from annihilation. Our upbringing has nothing to do with the purpose for which we have attained royalty. Drop the *childhood deprivation excuse* and move forward.

The *blame game excuse* needs to go. God asked Adam, *"Who told you that you were naked?"* Adam excused himself from answering by shifting the blame and saying, *"The woman that You gave me, she gave me to eat…,"* to which Eve excused herself by saying, *"The serpent deceived me, and I ate."* One excuse leads to another. We say, "I can't do what God is telling me to do because so and so did this." And so and so says, "Well, I can't do what God is telling me to do because such and such happened to me." Drop the *blame game excuse*! Excuses only set us up for defeat. God doesn't want to hear excuses. If He hears *excuses* He will *excuse* you. You will be excused from the benefits of the strong man's gospel, just like Elijah was excused from his prophetic ministry, and Saul's house was excused from kingly leadership over Israel.

The *know it all excuse* needs to go. Paul thought he was *it* when it came to the things of God – Philippians 3:5-6. He was of the *right birth* in the *right nation*. He went through the *right ceremonies* and the *right schools*. He had membership in the *right religious circles*, had *right behavior* and more than *right passion*. In Paul's mind there was none better than he. It was *his* way or the highway, and that with a whip! Brokenness was nowhere on his radar. But Paul's *know it all excuse* got run over on the road to Damascus when the Master of brokenness veered into his lane and hit him head on – Acts 9:1-19. He flushed all the *right stuff* behind his *know it all excuse* down the toilet like the dung that it was–Philippians 3:8. This man went on to demonstratively execute the intentions of the strong man's gospel in a way few others, if any, have. If the *know it all excuse* keeps brokenness out of our reach, we must flush all the *right stuff* propping up this excuse.

> **Paul's know it all excuse got run over on the road to Damascus when the Master of brokenness veered into his lane and hit him head on.**

Dropping all these excuses brings us to a point where *there is no excuse*. For the last character we consider has obliterated every excuse we could ever dream up! He is the One who introduced to us the strong man's gospel in Matthew 12. He is the One who came to place *this* gospel within us. If anyone legitimately had an excuse, this Man did. Jesus is the only one in this list who deserved none of the situations or circumstances hindering His ministry purpose. He had a legitimate right to *excuse* Himself from the call on His life. Yet Jesus rejected every excuse and with ultimate brokenness He embraced the very gospel He came to bring and pressed through every hindrance into victory. With His eyes fixed on the joy inside His mission, He endured what He had to endure to get this strong man's gospel in our hands – Hebrews 12:2. With His death and resurrection His mission was complete. He left us without an excuse to resist embracing the power of His brokenness. His work left us with no reason to neglect employing the power of the strong man's gospel in our lives. *"He himself has said, 'I will never leave you, nor will I forsake you,' so that we may confidently say, 'The Lord is my helper, I will not be afraid. What shall man do to me?'"* – Hebrews 13:5-6. We are without excuse!

In light of God's response to every excuse we have considered, we could conclude that He would say, "If you continue to make excuses for your position or your condition, you will not change. And if you do not change, your world will not change."

Embracing your excuses will not move *God* from His plan for your life, but embracing your excuses will move *you* from His plan for your life! His plan is for you to first embrace brokenness, a complete dependence on Him and His strength. Then His plan for you is to fulfill your mission by authentically operating in the strong man's gospel. God's plan to impact the world in which *you* live is for *Brokenness and the Strong Man's Gospel* to live through *you*!

> **Embracing your excuses will not move God from His plan for your life, but embracing your excuses will move you from His plan for your life!**

www.ingramcontent.com/pod-product-compliance
Ingram Content Group UK Ltd.
Pitfield, Milton Keynes, MK11 3LW, UK
UKHW022222230426
12048UKWH00016BA/1001